Value Chains and WTO Disputes

Aydin Baris Yildirim

Value Chains and WTO Disputes

Compliance at the dispute settlement mechanism

palgrave
macmillan

Aydin Baris Yildirim
World Trade Institute
Bern, Switzerland

ISBN 978-3-030-49093-5 ISBN 978-3-030-49094-2 (eBook)
https://doi.org/10.1007/978-3-030-49094-2

This Palgrave Macmillan imprint is published by the registered company Springer Nature Switzerland AG
The registered company address is: Gewerbestrasse 11, 6330 Cham, Switzerland

Dedicated to
Annem ve Babam'a

Acknowledgments

This book owes its existence to many individuals and institutions. I would first like to extend my thanks to Dirk De Bièvre and Arlo Poletti, my doctoral supervisors, whose help was invaluable in finishing my dissertation that served as the basis of this book. I started my doctoral training under their care and with their guidance I was able to finish successfully my program and received two very competitive grants that led to me finally finish this book. I could not ask for a more supportive team of supervisors and I will always remain grateful for their existence. I am also lucky enough to thank the jury members of my doctoral dissertation, Francesco Giumelli, Peter van Aelst, Peter Bursens, and Leonardo Baccini. Leo's help at the earlier stages was quite critical and his kind support later on helped me very much. Bernard Hoekman of the European University Institute, who was my mentor during my time there, was kind enough to provide feedback on an earlier draft which made all the difference.

I owe many thanks to my family and friends as well. My mom, dad, and my brothers were always on my mind during the past few years as I finished my dissertation, completed my fellowships, and finally wrote this book. Especially, my mom has been instrumental with her wonderful support over the years. My dear friend from Brussels Max helped me more times than I could count and Leo, Meron, and Kristof were so very helpful—I will never forget their help. My friends and colleagues from Florence and the EUI, especially Andrea, Silvia, Per, and Anna provided an amazing environment for me to finalize the book.

From an institutional standpoint, I extend my thanks to the University of Antwerp (UA) and the Research Fund of UA through which I was able to complete my doctoral program. The support system of the university was exceptional and beyond my supervisors and jury members, I was treated with utmost respect and care by the administration as well as the staff of UA. I would also like to extend my thanks to Robert Schuman Centre of the European University Institute where I wrote and drafted a significant part of the book. Through my time as a Max Weber Fellow, I was given a wonderful opportunity to finalize my book proposal and revise my manuscript for eventual submission. My colleagues and friends at RSC and the Max Weber program were extremely helpful and supportive throughout my fellowship and I will always remain thankful for their help for my career in general, and for this book's progression in particular. Lastly, I gratefully acknowledge funding from the European Union's Horizon 2020 research and innovation program under the Marie Skłodowska-Curie grant agreement PROSPER No. 842868. I was able to actually finish the book with the wonderful Marie Curie fellowship I was granted, which gave me all the time and energy to re-revise, submit, and finalize it.

It is also important to note that two publications inspired this book. The first one was published by the Review of International Organizations, titled. *The internationalization of production and the politics of compliance in WTO disputes*. The second one was published by the World Trade Review, titled *Firms' Integration into Value Chains and Compliance with Adverse WTO Panel Rulings*, which received the Best Graduate Student Paper Award in International Law by the International Studies Association (ISA). Lastly, this book is an extension of my doctoral dissertation and borrows much of its theoretical and empirical underpinnings. Empirical replication files can be found on my personal website—www.aydinbyildirim.com.

Contents

List of Figures

List of Tables

CHAPTER 1

Introduction

Abstract In an era where economic nationalist policies have been threatening the global trade order, the ability of the World Trade Organization (WTO) to maintain a liberal trade regime has come under intense scrutiny. Considering the decline of the WTO as a forum for negotiated trade liberalization, epitomized by the long-lasting impasse of the Doha Round, the importance of the WTO's judicial arm as a tool to maintaining a liberal trade regime has increased. In this backdrop, this chapter offers an overview of a novel theory that explains why and when governments are more likely to cooperate at the WTO dispute settlement and faster in complying with the rulings of the WTO panels. At the heart of this theory lies internationalization of production and cross-border value chains that shape the preferences domestic actors in trade policymaking—i.e., firms and sectors. I start by laying out the puzzle addressed in the book, give the readers an overview of how value chains pose a systemic counter force to the protectionist interests, and conclude by providing an outline of the book.

Keywords World Trade Organization · Dispute settlement · Compliance · Value chains

A. B. Yildirim, *Value Chains and WTO Disputes*,
https://doi.org/10.1007/978-3-030-49094-2_1

1.1 Cooperation and Discord in the International Trade Regime

In an era where economic populism has been threatening the global trade order, sustaining multilateral cooperation is becoming increasingly difficult. From the unilateral protectionist measures adopted by the Trump administration in the United States (US) to the British exit from the European Union (EU) that has fueled the mobilization of domestic isolationist interests, world trade regime is witnessing a number of challenges to maintaining previously made multilateral trade commitments. This book aims to shed light upon the conditions under which such challenges can be met and examine political-economic factors that explain World Trade Organization (WTO) members' behavior at the judicial arm of the WTO—i.e., the dispute settlement mechanism (DSM).

The decline of the WTO as a forum for negotiated trade liberalization, epitomized by the long-lasting impasse of the Doha Round, has increased the importance of the WTO's judicial arm as a tool to maintaining a liberal trade regime. Even in the face of blatant attacks on the legitimacy and the functioning of the WTO at the world stage, WTO Members increasingly rely on the DSM to resolve trade-related grievances—the number of disputes launched in 2017 and 2018 by the US, the EU, and other small and middle-sized economies is indicative of this trend.

Yet, as the need to sustain an open world economy is becoming more pressing, we know surprisingly little about WTO Members' behavior in response to international litigation. When are states more cooperative at the WTO? If they spend years drafting, ratifying, and implementing multilateral trade agreements, why do they sometimes refuse to abide by them? The literature on the institutional foundations of international cooperation suggests that the existence of mechanisms for the credible enforcement of agreed-upon rules is key to overcoming problems of cooperation that are typical of international trade relations (Keohane 1984; Martin 1992). A quasi-judicialized system of enforcement, such as the WTO DSM, should therefore be capable of performing the twofold function of preventing first and second-order compliance problems: creating disincentives for policies incompatible with WTO rules being adopted in the first place, and compelling members to bring their policies back into compliance with WTO rules whenever their wrongdoing is ascertained by the adjudicative body (Von Stein 2012).

However, we observe quite often that even in the face of authorized retaliation and direct financial penalties, WTO Members refuse to meet the demands of their trade partners. In other instances, the same WTO Members remarkably comply with their commitments in a swift manner without undue delays.

Consider the following examples: While the EU resisted to comply with the decision of the WTO panels in its long-standing dispute regarding imports of bananas from the African, Caribbean, and Pacific regions for some 15 years, a hotly debated dispute on imports of solar panels from China was resolved in less than two years (Chen 2015). It cost the EU approximately €200 million to keep the trade restrictions of bananas in place for so long and damaged its reputation as a law abiding WTO Member, creating a number of diplomatic tensions (Patterson 2001).[1] Similarly, in response to a dispute launched in 2001, the US resisted to meet the demands of its long time trade partner—Canada—regarding exports of softwood lumber for almost 5 years, despite authorized retaliation by the WTO. It costs Americans millions in legal fees, up to $200 million in retaliatory sanctions, and created a significant source of political tension with its Canadian neighbors (Lawrence 2007). In contrast, the US complied with the adverse panel ruling of the WTO regarding imports of steel products in 2002 in a matter of few months after the panel's decision was adopted, avoiding prolonged disputes and the risk of further economic and political damage.[2]

WTO Members' decisions to prolong disputes or quickly comply with the rulings of the dispute settlement panels have significant economic consequences. When raising protectionist trade barriers or eliminating existing trade restrictions, the distributive impact of such decisions empowers certain groups while hindering the political clout of others, both domestically and internationally. Following the example given above, when the US government decided to raise trade barriers in the steel sector in 2004, in a matter of months the US steel producers had a sharp surge in demand and almost doubled their revenue (Read 2005). In contrast,

[1] For a brief overview, see Patrick Barkham, "Banana Wars Explained," *The Guardian*, March 5, 1999. Accessed on February 12, 2017 via: https://www.theguardian.com/world/1999/mar/05/eu.wto3. See also Wall Street Journal, "WTO Allows Ecuador to Impose Sanctions in EU Banana Dispute," March 19, 2000. Accessed on February 12, 2017 via: https://www.wsj.com/articles/SB95345909977897928.

[2] See, *United States—Definitive Safeguard Measures on Imports of Certain Steel Products*.

consumers of steel such as automotive parts makers were suddenly cut off from their overseas supply lines and started to buy domestic steel at a higher price, increasing their cost of production some 20% (Francois and Baughman 2001). In the meantime, exporters of steel to the US from Europe or elsewhere lost an important part of their revenue stream.

This transfer of economic resources also has far-reaching political consequences. Domestically, empowered groups will find it easier to mobilize with their expanded resources, potentially shifting the domestic balance of interests in their favor. Thus, WTO Members' behavior at the WTO DSM would have direct implications for domestic societal interests. However, refusing to uphold international rules at the WTO DSM may have severe systematic repercussions on a global scale. One of the current debates on international trade raises the question of whether or not the current US administration under President Trump continuous its zealously protectionist behavior at the expense of US commitments at the WTO.[3] Indeed, policies that involve raising WTO-incompatible trade barriers or resisting to comply with the rulings of the panels would have far-reaching consequences for the global trade governance regime. For one, raising trade barriers can continue to invoke retaliatory threats from US trade partners, inciting a spiral of retaliation. Secondly, and more importantly, refusing to cooperate in the WTO DSM might heavily undermine the legitimacy of the WTO itself; the institution may be questioned due to its inability to deter opportunism, which would be regrettable since it was successful in preventing protectionism during the 2007–2008 financial crisis (Baccini and Kim 2012).

Examining the conditions under which WTO Members are more likely to comply with dispute settlement decisions is also theoretically interesting. Understanding how economic resources are distributed among societal groups due to international trade policies can shed light on how these groups may yield political influence with their resources. This in turn will help examine further developments in international political economy (IPE). Moreover, analyzing the conditions of sustained cooperation versus

[3] See, among others, John Plender, "Trump Trade Blind to Global Cost of Protectionism," *Financial Times*, 31 January 2017. Accessed on March 2, 2017 via: https://www.ft.com/content/2bee373a-e786-11e6-893c-082c54a7f539. Katie Allen, "Trump's Economic Policies: Protectionism, Low Taxes and Coal Mines," *The Guardian*, November 9, 2016. Accessed on March 2, 2017 via: https://www.theguardian.com/us-news/2016/nov/09/trumps-economic-policies-protectionism-low-taxes-and-coal-mines.

discord in international trade governance can give us a general clue about cooperation in international relations.

Accordingly, this book aims to answer the following research question: *under what conditions do WTO Members swiftly comply with adverse WTO panel rulings?*

In order to account for such variation in WTO Member behavior, a broad examination of trade policymaking is needed, one that takes into account societal trade-related interests as well as the growing internationalization of production. While the former has received significant attention in the field of politics and international relations (IR), the latter needs much more attention. Scholars have extensively demonstrated that the demands of mobilized domestic groups and their respective power are the primary force that shapes state policies (e.g., Milner 1987; Moravcsik 1997; Goldstein and Martin 2000; Mansfield and Milner 2017). According to this conventional view, policymakers are bound to the demands of their domestic constituencies and act by steering a course between potentially conflicting interests. However, even though the impact of domestic actors on economic policies has been explored in detail, explaining their impact on WTO Member governments' responses to litigation has been limited at best.

In order to account for the variation in the time it takes WTO Members to comply with panel rulings, this book proposes a novel theoretical argument that focuses on the importance of internationalization of production on trade policymaking. It highlights how varying degrees of integration into networks of production shapes the preferences of domestic political-economic actors—i.e., firms and sectors—which ultimately shapes the behavior of WTO Member governments in response to litigation.

Over the last few decades, a growing trend in the field of IPE have brought about a rich and growing scholarly work that focuses on the complex, interconnected, and yet geographically dispersed patterns of trade and production, referred broadly as "global value chains" (e.g., Baldwin 2012; Elms and Low 2013) or "global production networks" (e.g., Levy 2008). This nascent literature has highlighted a particular type of internationalization that focuses on the activity of firms that increasingly engage in productions across different countries where they produce various parts and components before delivering a final product or service. These changes in patterns of trade, production, and distribution activities of firms—collectively referred as "integration into value chains" in this study—have systematically transformed the structure of world trade, where a state's comparative advantage—namely, productivity—and competitiveness increasingly lie in its degree of integration into these chains of production. Illustratively, the United Nations Conference in Trade and Development (UNCTAD) recently reported that almost 60% of world trade now consists of trade in intermediate goods and services (UNCTAD 2013) while it is estimated that more than 80% of merchandise exports and imports of pivotal international economic players now takes place within networks of production and distribution (e.g., Bernard et al. 2009). In consequence, firms and sectors that are active in value chains now engage in value-added trade across borders, and rely extensively on foreign inputs for their productions, creating an additional demand for trade liberalization.

Current developments in US trade policy reveals the importance of internationalization in triggering the political mobilization of integrated firms and their sector associations. Although at first sight it might be perceived that firms' integration could not stop the protectionist policies helmed by the Trump administration, firms and sectors active along supply chains have been mobilizing with speed and fiercely opposing the administration's protectionist policies. Take the US steel sector for instance. In response to the recent imposition of retaliatory tariffs from several US trade partners in the steel and aluminum production sector, highly integrated US steel manufacturers and automotive companies, such as NLMK US, the California Steel Industries, and the Alliance of Automotive Manufacturers, protested against the measures and later petitioned to the Department of Commerce in order to be exempt from the duties raised.[4] Moreover, American Institute for International Steel resorted to domestic litigation and filed an action in the US Court of International Trade, challenging the constitutionality of the Trump administration's use of Section 232—i.e., the section of the law allegedly allows the president to enact tariff duties.[5]

[4] See for instance, Richard Lardner, "Rising Backlash as US Firms Seek Trump's Steel Tariff Waiver," *The Associated Press*. Accessed on 22 August 2018 via: https://globalnews.ca/news/4359349/rising-backlash-as-us-firms-seek-trumps-steel-tariff-waiver/.

[5] See for instance, Shawn Donnan and Vladimir Waldemir, "Industry Backlash to Trump Tariffs Grows with Legal Challenge," *Financial Times*. Accessed on 10 September 2018 via: https://www.ft.com/content/7e35b986-7a20-11e8-bc55-50daf11b720d.

Similarly, import-dependent firms have shown similar agility regarding their political mobilization in response to threats to their operations. On December 2016, President Trump announced his plan to introduce a so-called border adjustment tax that would have increased the cost of exports to the US by up to 20% across the board on many goods and services (Bown 2017). Following his announcement, many American firms that heavily depend on imports immediately started to mobilize against it and formed a coalition to stop it from going forward.[6] Chief Executive Officers (CEO's) of Walmart, Target, Best Buy, GAP, among others, have called on the US administration to scrap the tax, claiming that it would wipe their profits out, as opposed to import-competing groups who expressed their clear support.[7] While it is too early to say how successful these attempts will be, one thing is clear, firms and sectors integrated into value chains—and rely on foreign imports—(re)act swiftly to pursue their trade policy preferences—a point I return to in the conclusion.

Internationalization of production has far-reaching implications for the politics of WTO dispute settlement. In a world increasingly characterized by international value chains, WTO Members now face additional pressure from domestic actors (i.e., firms and sectors integrated into value chains) to keep their trade liberalization commitments in place. The political activity of these actors essentially increases the domestic demand for trade liberalization, which in turn increases policymakers' incentives to resist the demands of protectionist interests. In line with this logic, I posit that the time until WTO Members comply with the rulings of the WTO panel is much shorter when a dispute affects firms active in sectors that are integrated into value chains. In such disputes, these actors are triggered to mobilize and seek to remove these barriers that restrict their cross-border trade. Disruption to their cross-border trade gives them an incentive to

[6] Corinne Ruff, "Wal-Mart, Target, NRF Lead Retail Industry Coalition to Fight Border Tax," *Retail Dive*, February 2, 2017. Accessed on March 10, 2017 via: http://www.retaildive.com/news/wal-mart-target-nrf-lead-retail-industry-coalition-to-fight-border-tax/435359/.

[7] Ylan Mui, "Trump Gets an Earful About a Tax That Retailers Call 'Risky and Unproven'," *CNBC News*, February 15, 2017. Accessed on March 10, 2017 via: http://www.cnbc.com/2017/02/15/border-adjustment-retailers-tell-trump-about-risky-and-unproven-tax.html. Lucinda Shen, "These 21 Companies Back the GOP's Proposed Border Adjustment Tax," Fortune Finance, February 13, 2017. Accessed on April 1, 2017 via: http://fortune.com/2017/02/13/donald-trump-border-adjustment-tax-support/.

lobby for the removal of trade barriers targeted in WTO litigation, and their mobilization increases the political weight of pro-trade advocates in the economies of defendant WTO Members.

When a trade dispute touches upon firms that are not—or only weakly—integrated into value chains, the political conflict will be of the kind traditionally depicted (i.e., between exporters and import competitors). In such a scenario where the domestic political equilibrium in the form of maintaining trade liberalization commitments is disrupted, policymakers have incentives to cheat on their trade liberalization commitments at the WTO. However, the political conflict changes in nature when a dispute touches upon domestic actors that are highly integrated into these chains of production. These economic actors oppose the WTO-challenged measures because such goods are critical components of their production processes. Therefore, the removal of WTO-incompatible trade barriers will not only be supported by those exporters that fear foreign market closure through retaliation, but also by those who wish to exploit the opportunity to access imports of intermediate goods more cheaply. All things being equal, one should therefore expect a dispute affecting firms and sectors highly integrated into regional and global value chains to engender a political dynamic that is more prone to result in swifter compliance than a dispute targeting firms only weakly integrated into value chains.

Essentially, the initiation of a WTO dispute against firms highly integrated into value chains steers the domestic balance of interests in favor of maintaining trade open, at least relative to a scenario in which these pro-trade actors' mobilization is absent. Under these circumstances, policymakers in defendant WTO Members now face a twin pressure to implement panel rulings in a swift manner; the trade-liberalizing responses to WTO legal challenges are therefore faster.

1.2 The Puzzle

The WTO regulates approximately $20 trillion in goods and services and its judicial arm, the DSM, aims to ensure WTO Members resolve their disputes in a swift, efficient manner. This legal system functions in a way that is similar to an inter-state court where WTO Members can challenge the trade policies of other members they deem to be WTO-illegal. The primary objective of the system is to resolve disputes via consultations between members but in cases where disputants do not agree on a settlement, the DSM provides adjudicating panels with expert panelists and a standing appeals mechanism—the Appellate Body (AB)—that render legally binding rulings (WTO 2004). In adjudicated disputes in which parties cannot reach a settlement, the DSM can authorize retaliation that can compel WTO Members to bring their policies back into compliance with WTO rules whenever their wrongdoing is ascertained by the dispute settlement panels (Von Stein 2012). Born out of the General Agreement on Tariff and Trade (GATT), the WTO DSM has been heralded as a unique system that represents "the greatest amount of legalisation that we know at the multilateral level" (Shaffer et al. 2016, p. 24).

There have been over 500 disputes brought to the WTO since its inception in 1995, and a large majority of them have been resolved (Alter 2003; Chaudoin et al. 2016). It is reported that roughly half of the disputes at the WTO are settled in bilateral consultations, and for the remaining disputes that reached the panels stage of the DSM, 90% have reportedly resulted in compliance (WTO 2016). Yet, a closer look reveals that this prima facie compliance record is misleading, and that the behavior of WTO Members in complying with the decisions of the panels varies dramatically across disputes that they are involved in. In other words, compliance with adverse panel rulings varies greatly in terms of how long the defendant WTO Members take to meet their trade partners' demands and bring their domestic legislation in line with their WTO commitments (Young 2010; Davey 2005).

Take the US for instance. Following a successful legal challenge from a trade partner at the WTO, the US takes 28 months on average to comply with an adverse ruling. This means that from the date of circulation of a panel report, the time it takes for the US to comply with the ruling and change its WTO-illegal domestic policy is around 2 years, adjusting for the administrative time it takes the panels to circulate and adopt their reports. Yet, while the US has reached a resolution in the past on some disputes in a matter of days (e.g., EC copyrights dispute), it refused to comply in certain disputes for over seven years (e.g., the disputes involving the Byrd Amendment that increased US import duties).

This example involving the US is in no way an exception. Almost all WTO Members have demonstrated a great variation in the time it would take them to comply with the rulings of the WTO panels. Table 1.1 shows that the US, EU, members of the Organization for Economic Cooperation and Development (OECD), and developing countries all

Table 1.1 WTO Members' record of compliance

WTO Members	*Time until compliance with WTO panel rulings (in months)*		
	Minimum	*Average*	*Maximum*
USA	1	28	178
EU	1	25	149
OECD members	1	23	178
Developing countries	1	16	61

Source Dispute Settlement Database (DSD) compiled by the author

demonstrate willingness to swiftly implement the decision of the panels at times, while also displaying remarkable resistance to compliance at other times.

This variation in the time it takes for WTO Members to implement WTO panel rulings is both important and puzzling. When a WTO Member refuses to bring its policies in line with its WTO commitments, the policy in questions continues to have a significant (economic) redistributive impact. For instance, after raising the aforementioned import barriers via the Byrd Amendment, US-based firms and sectors that benefited from the trade barrier—especially that produce bearings, metals, and household items—reportedly gained over $250 million every year for seven years while retailers, importers, and consumers were actually incurring this rise in import and production costs (CEC 2004; Rus 2007).[8]

Similarly, the aforementioned border tariffs imposed by the US administration on steel and aluminum products are likely to be both disruptive and WTO-inconsistent according to several analyses.[9] Both industry

[8] For an overview of the damage caused by the Byrd Amendment to the US sectors, consumers (as well as to the foreign exporters), see Daniella Markheim, "Time to Repeal the Byrd Amendment," The Heritage Foundation Trade Report, October 2005. Accessed on 2 February 2017 via: http://www.heritage.org/trade/report/time-repeal-the-byrd-amendment.

[9] See Chad Bown, *Trump's Steel and Aluminum Tariffs: How WTO Retaliation Typically Works*. Peterson Institute for International Economics, 2018. Accessed on 1 September 2018 via: https://piie.com/blogs/trade-investment-policy-watch/trumps-steel-and-aluminum-tariffs-how-wto-retaliation-typically. See also Lulu Garcia-Navarro, *The WTO and Trump's Tariffs*, a Conversation with Jennifer Hillman, National Public Radio (NPR). Accessed on 12 September 2018 via: https://text.npr.org/s.php?sId=616551960.

groups and experts have warned that if this particular barrier is found to be incompatible with WTO rules and the US government refuses to withdraw the measure, the authorized retaliatory sanctions will be incurred by exporters to the US, the users of the taxed products, as well as the American public.[10]

Examining WTO Members' compliance behavior is also theoretically interesting. Above all, it is counterintuitive to observe resistance to compliance from WTO Members. Governments have paid hundreds of thousands of dollars in legal fees (Bown and Reynolds 2014) and millions of dollars as a result of authorized retaliation (Bonomo 2014) in cases of non-compliance so far. Yet, all the direct financial costs and the reputational costs of non-abidance still do not prevent WTO Members from refusing to uphold their promises. More importantly, the growing literature on the WTO has yet to explain the conditions under which governments are more compliant. Proposed explanations as to why and when governments are more or less rule abiding at the WTO DSM fail short on explaining the behavior of many WTO Members and have not accounted for the dispute settlement behavior of governments in the large majority of disputes.

1.3 Proposed Explanations and the Argument in Brief

In order to account for the variance in WTO Members' record of compliance, scholars have shed light on a number of plausible factors that can be grouped into two domains: ***horizontal*** state-to-state explanations, and ***vertical*** sources of influence that examine the impact of domestic groups on states' international policies. Horizontally, power asymmetries between the litigants and the threat of retaliation wielded by the complainants have been proposed as the primary reason why WTO Members show willingness to comply (or resist meeting their trade partners' demands) at the WTO DSM (Mavroidis 2012; Bown 2004; Guzman and Simmons 2005).

From the perspective of "vertical" sources of influence, scholars have examined domestic political institutions, i.e., whether or not democratic WTO Members are more rule-abiding (Dixon 1993; Slaughter

[10] See Shawn Donnan and Vladimir Waldemir, "Industry Backlash to Trump Tariffs Grows with Legal Challenge," *Financial Times*. Accessed on 10 September 2018 via: https://www.ft.com/content/7e35b986-7a20-11e8-bc55-50daf11b720d.

1995), and the role of mobilized interest groups, i.e., the preferences of mobilized trade-related interests in domestic economies that shape the behavior of WTO Members' governments (Goldstein and Martin 2000). Among the two the latter has especially received increased attention within the last few decades (Milner 1987; Goldstein and Steinberg 2008; Young 2010; Poletti and De Bièvre 2014) and has largely focused on the mechanisms through which domestic interests mobilize and achieve their policy objectives. In the context of the WTO DSM, it has been argued that WTO Members are more rule-abiding in general and comply with the rulings of the WTO panels when the affected domestic actors favor this outcome. Assuming that policymakers are susceptible to pressures from their constituencies, trade policy outcomes are argued to be in line with the preferences of the group that has more political clout.

I share these assumptions about the nature of trade policymaking. I too argue that domestic actors—i.e., firms and sectors—primarily shape the trade policy preferences of governments. Yet, I go beyond these explanations and consider for the first time the implications of internationalization of production on the domestic politics of compliance. The literature in international political economy has attempted to incorporate the impact of value chains on trade policymaking in the context of preferential trade agreements (PTAs), but there has not been any examination into the impact of these networks on the behavior of WTO Members at the WTO dispute settlement level, even though there is high plausibility that integration into value chains increases firms' and sectors' tendencies to tackle trade-disruptive WTO-illegal barriers (Antràs and Staiger 2012; Orefice and Rocha 2014).

This book aims to accomplish precisely that task. I argue that internationalization of production has important implications for the study of trade policy in general, and for the study of WTO dispute settlement in particular. Broadly speaking, the expansion of production networks increases demand for trade without disruptive barriers. This is because firms that are integrated into value chains engage in value added with their affiliates, subsidiaries, and suppliers. They prefer smooth operation of their supply chains and would want to avoid imposition of trade barriers that would disrupt their productions. Thus, because the internationalization of production makes companies increasingly dependent on imports of intermediate goods for their production process, maintaining low domestic trade barriers becomes a valued political objective for them to avoid significantly increased production costs.

As such, these firms' political activity increases the pro-trade constituencies in domestic economies and changes the constellation of interest in trade policymaking across WTO Member economies. A traditional account of trade policy is expected to engender a political conflict between two sets of actors: export-oriented firms and sectors that favor trade liberalization, and their pro-protectionist counterparts that are mainly import competing (Hiscox 2001). The first set of actors stands to gain from the increased market access opportunities that trade liberalization can bring about, while the second stands to lose from it because of the greater exposure to foreign competition in domestic markets. However, this distinction which has been extensively used no longer accurately reflects the reality of contemporary trade politics in either advanced or emerging economies. In a world economy increasingly characterized by internationalization of production, the preferences, patterns of political mobilization, and influence of firms and the sectors they populate that rely on income generated from the import of intermediate products for their production process need to be added to the equation (Jensen et al. 2015).

In the past, producers in developed countries bought or produced the bulk of their products and inputs domestically, and then traded finished goods among themselves. Since the 1990s, these producers have redefined their core competencies and turned their attention to innovation and product strategy, marketing, and to the highest value-added segments of manufacturing and services. At the same time, they have outsourced labor-intensive, lower-value-added operations to lower-income countries (Gereffi et al. 2005, p. 79), creating value chains across boundaries.

From the perspective of the domestic political economy of trade, the most important implication of the increasing relevance of these production networks in the world economy is that international trade flows are no longer almost exclusively about trade in finished goods, but also largely about trade in intermediate goods. Illustratively, trade in intermediates accounts for over two-thirds of total imports for the majority of the OECD members (Johnson and Noguera 2012), while it is estimated that more than 80% of merchandise exports and imports of pivotal international economic players now takes place within networks of production and distribution (e.g., Bernard et al. 2009).

This type of internationalization of production has far-reaching implications for the politics of WTO dispute settlement. In a world increasingly characterized by international value chains, WTO Members now face additional pressure from domestic actors (i.e., firms and sectors integrated into value chains) to keep their trade liberalization commitments in place. The political activity of these actors essentially increases the domestic demand for trade liberalization, which in turn increases policymakers' incentives to resist the demands of protectionist interests. In line with this logic, I posit that the time until WTO Members comply with the rulings of the WTO panel is much shorter when a dispute affects firms that are integrated into value chains. In such disputes, these actors are triggered to mobilize and seek to remove these barriers that restrict their cross-border trade, primarily through in coalition with other firms with similar interests in their sector. Disruption to their cross-border trade gives them an incentive to lobby for the removal of trade barriers targeted in WTO litigation, and their mobilization increases the political weight of pro-trade advocates in the economies of defendant WTO Members.

When a trade dispute touches upon firms that are not—or only weakly—integrated into value chains, the political conflict will be of the kind traditionally depicted (i.e., between exporters and import competitors). In such a scenario where the domestic political equilibrium in the form of maintaining trade liberalization commitments is disrupted, policymakers have incentives to cheat on their trade liberalization commitments at the WTO. However, the political conflict changes in nature when a dispute touches upon domestic actors that are highly integrated into these chains of production. These economic actors oppose the WTO-challenged measures because such goods are critical components of their production processes. Therefore, the removal of WTO-incompatible trade barriers will not only be supported by those exporters that fear foreign market closure through retaliation, but also by those who wish to exploit the opportunity to access imports of intermediate goods more cheaply.

All things being equal, one should therefore expect a dispute affecting firms highly integrated into regional and global value chains to engender a political dynamic that is more prone to result in swifter compliance than a dispute targeting firms only weakly integrated into value chains.

Essentially, the initiation of a WTO dispute against firms highly integrated into value chains steers the domestic balance of interests in favor of maintaining trade open, at least relative to a scenario in which these pro-trade actors' mobilization is absent. Under these circumstances, policymakers in defendant WTO Members now face a twin pressure to implement panel rulings in a swift manner; the trade-liberalizing responses to WTO legal challenges are therefore faster.

1.4 The Structure of the Book

This book proceeds as follows: I start the following section by reviewing the literature and presenting my argument. I first critically examine the literature on international relations, trade policy, WTO dispute settlement, and value chains. In doing so, I highlight the contributions of this study to these different literatures. I then present my argument in detail, elaborate on the assumptions I make, and clarify the concepts I use. I give a detailed account of the theoretical expectations that will be tested in the following sections, i.e., how and when domestic actors' integration into value chains decrease the time until WTO Members comply with adverse panel rulings.

In the third and the fourth section, I lay out two empirical parts in which I conduct my analyses. These two sections both aim to answer the above-mentioned research question and complement each other to give a detailed picture of not only *why* but also *how* integration into value chains decreases the time until WTO Members' comply with adverse panel rulings. Here I highlight my critical rational approach to social scientific phenomena (Popper 1934) and conduct analyses based on the most appropriate and useful techniques to answer my research question by subjecting it to rigorous testing via two different methods. In Section 3, I present an aggregate examination of WTO Members' responses to litigation at the DSM. I take into account all of the disputes tabled at the WTO that resulted in a panel ruling and examine all defendant WTO Members' responses to litigation. I demonstrate that defendant WTO Members much more quickly comply when targeted measures involve sectors highly integrated into value chains. Using Cox survival analysis that aims to explain the "death" of disputes, I show that higher integration of targeted sectors decreases the time until WTO Members implement panel rulings across the board.

In Section 4, I complement my statistical analysis with case studies. Having demonstrated the impact of value chain integration on WTO Members' propensity to meet their trade partners' demands at the WTO, I aim to show in this section *how* domestic actors actually mobilize and press their preferences to policymakers. The aim of this section is to trace the mechanisms through which domestic actors influence the behavior of WTO Members at the DSM. I specifically demonstrate how US and

Canadian firms integrated into value chains mobilize, enter into coalitions through their sector associations, and lobby for the removal of trade barriers in response to WTO litigation.

Following the analyses, I finalize the study with a conclusion that summarizes my main findings, provides policy advice, future research prospects, and the implications of my research in the context of trade tensions that have been growing in the past few years. I highlight the importance of my research for the future understanding of trade politics and how the logic I postulate applies to firms' and sectors' trade policy preferences beyond the WTO.

References

Alter, K. 2003. Resolving or Exacerbating Disputes? The WTO's New Dispute Resolution System. *International Affairs* 79 (4): 783–800.

Antràs, Pol, and Robert W. Staiger. 2012. Offshoring and the Role of Trade Agreements. *American Economic Review* 102 (7): 3140–3183.

Baccini, L., and S.Y. Kim. 2012. Preventing Protectionism: International Institutions and Trade Policy. *The Review of International Organizations* 7 (4): 369–398.

Baldwin, R. 2012. Global Supply Chains: Why They Emerged, Why They Matter, and Where They Are Going. Working Paper 2012-01, Fung Global Institute, Hong Kong.

Bernard, A., B. Jensen, and P.K. Schott. 2009. Importers, Exporters, and Multinationals: A Portrait of Firms in the U.S. That Trade Goods. In *Producer Dynamics*, ed. Timothy Dunne, J. Bradford Jensen and Mark J. Roberts. Chicago: University of Chicago Press.

Bonomo, D. 2014. Hitting Where It Hurts: Retaliation Requests in the WTO. VoxEU, Centre for Economic and Policy Research. Available at http://voxeu.org/article/retaliation-wto. Accessed on June 22, 2017.

Bown, C. 2004. On the Economic Success of GATT/WTO Dispute Settlement. *The Review of Economics and Statistics* 86 (3): 811–823.

Bown, C. 2017. Will the Proposed U.S. Border Tax Provoke WTO Retaliation From Trading Partners? Peterson Institute for International Economics Policy Paper. Available at https://piie.com/publications/policy-briefs/will-proposed-us-border-tax-provoke-wto-retaliation-trading-partners. Accessed on June 21, 2017.

Bown, C., and K. Reynolds. 2014. Trade Flows and Trade Disputes. Policy Research Working Paper 6979. Development Research Team, World Bank, Washington.

Chaudoin, S., J. Kucik, and K. Pelc. 2016. Do WTO Disputes Actually Increase Trade? *International Studies Quarterly* 0: 1–13. Advanced online publication. Available at http://isq.oxfordjournals.org/content/early/2016/04/15/isq.sqw009.

Chen, Yu. 2015. EU-China Solar Panels Trade Dispute: Settlement and challenges to the EU. European Institute for Asian Studies. Available at http://www.eias.org/eu-asia-at-a-glance/eu-china-solar-panels-trade-dispute-settlement-and-challenges-for-the-eu-june-2015/. Accessed on February 10, 2017.

Commission of the European Communities (CEC). 2004. US Byrd Amendment—WTO Says Eight WTO Members May Retaliate Against the US—Joint Press statement by Brazil, Canada, Chile, the EU, India, Japan, Korea, and Mexico. MEMO IP/04/1055, August 31.

Davey, A. 2005. Evaluating WTO Dispute Settlement: What Results Have Been Achieved Through Consultations and Implementation of Panel Reports? Research Paper 05-19. Chicago, IL: College of Law, University of Illinois.

Dixon, W.J. 1993. Democracy and the Management of International Conflict. *Journal of Conflict Resolution* 37 (1): 42–68.

Elms, D., and P. Low. 2013. Global Value Chains in a Changing World, Introduction, Switzerland: World Trade Organization. Available at https://www.wto.org/english/res_e/booksp_e/aid4tradeglobalvalue13_e.pdf. Accessed on June 20, 2020.

Francois, J., and L. Baughman. 2001. Estimated Economic Effects of Proposed Import Relief Remedies for Steel. Report Prepared by Trade Partnership Worldwide LLC. Available at http://tradepartnership.com/reports/estimated-economic-effects-of-proposed-import-relief-remedies-for-steel-2001/.

Gereffi, G., J. Humphrey, and T. Sturgeon. 2005. The Governance of Global Value Chains. *Review of International Political Economy* 12 (1): 78–104.

Goldstein, Judith, and Lisa L. Martin. 2000. Legalization, Trade Liberalization, and Domestic Politics: A Cautionary Note. *International Organization* 54 (3): 603–632.

Goldstein, J., and R. Steinberg. 2008. Negotiate or Litigate? Effects of WTO Judicial Delegation on US Trade Politics. *Law and Contemporary Problems* 71 (1): 257–282.

Guzman, A., and B. Simmons. 2005. Power Plays and Capacity Constraints: The Selection of Defendants in World Trade Organization Disputes. *Journal of Legal Studies* 34 (2): 557–598.

Hiscox, M.J. 2001. Class Versus Industry Cleavages: Inter-Industry Factor Mobility and the Politics of Trade. *International Organization* 55: 1–46.

Jensen, B., D. Quinn, and S. Weymouth. 2015. The Influence of Firm Global Supply Chains and Foreign Currency Undervaluations on US Trade Disputes. *International Organization* 69: 913–947.

Johnson, R.C., and G. Noguera. 2012. Accounting for Intermediates: Production Sharing and Trade in Value Added. *Journal of International Economics* 86 (2): 224–236.

Keohane, R. 1984. *After Hegemony: Cooperation and Discord in the World Political Economy*. Princeton, NJ: Princeton University Press.

Lawrence, R. 2007. The United States and the WTO Dispute Settlement System. Council on Foreign Relations, Greenberg Center for Geoeconomic Studies Special Report. Available at https://www.cfr.org/report/united-states-and-wto-dispute-settlement-system. Accessed on June 19, 2017.

Levy, D.L. 2008. Political Contestation in Global Production Networks. *Academy of Management Review* 33 (4): 943–963.

Mansfield, E., and H. Milner. 2017. The Domestic Politics of Preferential Trade Agreements in Hard Times. *World Trade Review*. https://doi.org/10.1017/S1474745617000428.

Martin, L. 1992. Interests, Power, and Multilateralism. *International Organization* 46 (4): 765–792.

Mavroidis, Petros. 2012. On Compliance in the WTO: Enforcement Among Unequal Disputants. Briefing Paper No. 4. Geneva: CUTS International.

Milner, H. 1987. Resisting the Protectionist Temptation: Industry and the Making of Trade Policy in France and the United States During the 1970s. *International Organization* 41 (4): 639–665.

Moravcsik, A. 1997. Taking Preferences Seriously: A Liberal Theory of International Politics. *International Organization* 51 (4): 513–553.

Orefice, G., and N. Rocha. 2014. Deep Integration and Production Networks: An Empirical Analysis. *The World Economy* 37 (1): 106–136.

Patterson, E. 2001. The US-EU Banana Dispute. *American Society of International Law (ASIL) Insight Paper* 6: 4. Available at https://www.asil.org/insights/volume/6/issue/4/us-eu-banana-dispute. Accessed on January 2, 2017.

Poletti, A., and D. De Bièvre. 2014. Political Mobilization, Veto Players, and WTO Litigation: Explaining European Union Responses in Trade Disputes. *Journal of European Public Policy* 21 (8): 1181–1198.

Popper, K. 1934. *The Logic of Scientific Inquiry*. London: Routledge.

Read, R. 2005. The EU-US WTO Steel Dispute: Political Economy of Protection and the Efficacy of the WTO Dispute Settlement Understanding. In *The WTO and the Regulation of International Trade: Recent Trade Disputes Between the European Union and the United States*, ed. Nicholas Perdikis and Robert Read, 135–175. Cheltenham : Edward Elgar.

Rus, T. 2007. The Short, Unhappy life of the Byrd Amendment, N.Y.U. *Journal of Legislation and Public Policy* 10 (2): 427–443.

Shaffer, G., M. Elsig, and S. Puig. 2016. The Law and Politics of WTO Dispute Settlement. In *The Politics of International Law*, ed. Wayne Sandholtz and Christopher Whytock. Oxford: Oxford University Press.

Slaughter, A. 1995. International Law in a World of Liberal States. *European Journal of International Law* 6 (1): 503–538.

United Nations Conference on Trade and Development (UNCTAD). 2013. World Investment Report, Global Value Chains: Investment and Trade for Development. United Nations Publication: Switzerland. Available at https://unctad.org/en/PublicationsLibrary/wir2013_en.pdf. Accessed on June 20, 2020.

Von Stein, J. 2012. The Engines of Compliance. In *Synthesizing Insights from International Law and International Relations*, ed. Jeffrey Dunoff and Mark Pollack. Cambridge: Cambridge University Press.

World Trade Organization. 2004. *Handbook on the WTO Dispute Settlement System*. Cambridge: Cambridge University Press.

World Trade Organization. 2016. *Resolving Trade Disputes Between WTO Members*. Geneva: Switzerland. https://www.wto.org/english/thewto_e/20y_e/dispute_brochure20y_e.pdf. Accessed on June 20, 2020.

Young, A.R. 2010. Effective Multilateralism on Trial: EU Compliance with WTO Law. In *The EU's Presence in International Organisations*, ed. S. Blavoukos and D. Bourantonis, vol. 67, 114–131. European Union Series: Routledge advances in European politics. Abingdon, UK: Routledge.

CHAPTER 2

Theorizing Cooperation in International Trade and the WTO DSM

Abstract What is the impact of firms' value chain integration on their trade preferences? In this chapter, I review the scholarship on trade policy, value chains, and compliance at the WTO dispute settlement. I theorize on the potential impact of value chains on firms' and sectors' political mobilization over trade policies in general, and over WTO dispute settlement rulings in particular. I propose that WTO Members' cooperative behavior at the dispute settlement is shaped by domestic interests' demands, which in turn is significantly shaped by their integration into value chains. Firms that are integrated into value chain networks have clear preferences over free trade to avoid disruption to their production processes and imports that they rely on. All things being equal, the combination of exporters that seek market access and the integrated import-dependent firms' mobilization changes the domestic balance of interests in favor of trade liberalization and swift compliance with WTO panel rulings.

Keywords Firms · Cooperation · Trade policy · International institutions

A. B. Yildirim, *Value Chains and WTO Disputes*,
https://doi.org/10.1007/978-3-030-49094-2_2

2.1 State of the Art: Situating the Study in a Broader Context

This research broadly speaks to the literature that aims to explain and understand the extent to which international rules and institutions can constrain states' behavior. The phenomenon I examine—i.e., WTO Members' behavior at the WTO DSM—is, above all, about the implications of an international institution, the WTO, and the rules governed by this institution. I therefore follow the literature that came be to be known as neoliberal institutional political science (e.g., Krasner 1983), in which scholars mainly put forward the idea that institutions enhance the likelihood of cooperation by reducing transaction costs, generating information, reducing uncertainty, and increasing expectations of compliance (Axelrod and Keohane 1985; Dunoff and Pollack 2012), or put simply "international cooperation is developed and sustained by international institutions" (Barrett 2007, p. 19).

The key insights developed within the institutionalist political science scholarship have engendered a rich literature that examines the foundations of cooperation in global trade governance.[1] A number of scholars have attempted to explain if and how governments are more likely to uphold their trade liberalization commitments in the presence of the WTO (e.g., Baccini and Kim 2012; Zangl 2008), broadly noting that the presence of the WTO help governments promote their cooperative efforts while limiting the space for opportunistic behavior.

In order to shed light upon the underlying mechanism of sustaining cooperation, a large majority of studies have focused on "horizontal," i.e., state-to-state, and "vertical," i.e., within-state sources of influence to explain why states follow or resist international rules. Works in the "horizontal" strand adopted a rationalist view and stated that international rule abidance rests on three elements: reciprocity, reputation, and retaliation (e.g., Guzman 2008), applying game theoretic models and prisoner's dilemma payoff structures to international affairs (Axelrod 1984; Snidal 1985). Considering states as being in an iterated game, a government does not have an incentive to renege on an agreement because the interaction is continuous; therefore, the "shadow of the future" prevents states from breaking their promises. Secondly, some proposed that states abide by their international commitments because they value their reputation in

[1] See Poletti (2017) for an overview.

upholding international law (Brewster 2012). A reputation for continuous non-compliance may lead to the exclusion of the unreliable state partner from future agreements and cause further decay in a given system because promises appear to be untenable (Keohane 1984). Thirdly, some argued that incentives to cheat on given promises are prevented by the threat of retaliation. States face retaliatory pressures from other states, pressures that might take the form of "soft" pressure, e.g., diplomatic (Conti 2010) or "hard" pressure, e.g., economic sanctions or military intervention.

Although these horizontal sources of influence on international rule abidance have been examined in the context of a range of international issues, such as environment (e.g., Bernhagen 2008; Barret 2007), human rights (e.g., Hafner-Burton 2005), humanitarian law (e.g., Morrow 2007), and trade (e.g., Bown 2009), the literature started to move toward taking into account "vertical" sources of influence, i.e., domestic factors (Koremenos 2012, p. 74), incorporating information "on the demands of organized groups and their relative power in society, as a fundamental force driving state policy" (Moravcsik 2012, p. 93).

The "vertical" analysis of international affairs has led a large literature that examines how domestic politics impact international politics and how international politics, in turn, affect domestic politics. Most of the works in the field borrowed from Putnam's (1988) "two-level game" as well as Keohane and Nye's (1977) "complex interdependence" where policymakers bargain with their international counterparts and, at the same time, negotiate with domestic actors—both at home and abroad. The growing literature in this strand has analyzed the potential causes of (non) compliance with international human rights law (e.g., Hathaway 2002; Simmons 2009), environmental law (e.g., Dai 2008), and international trade law (e.g., Milner 1997; von Stein 2012). Works in this strand examined whether or not democracies are more rule abiding (Simmons 2000; Slaughter 1995), if domestic pro-compliance constituencies foster cooperative behavior (Dai 2005) and whether or not legislative constraints at the domestic level can hamper the ability of states to foster cooperation (Mansfield et al. 2007; Martin 2000; Young 2010).

The broader contribution of this book is attempted at this particular subfield. I contribute to these works by examining the domestic foundations of international cooperation in the global trade regime and try to further sharpen our understanding of states' behavior in international fora, *in casu* the WTO.

More particularly, I contribute to this literature by applying an international political economy approach and arguing that the preferences of domestic actors, who mobilize and press their policy objectives, ultimately explain WTO Members' behavior. Firms that are affected by a WTO dispute mobilize through their sectors and bring forward their policy preferences. Assuming that politicians are support-maximizers who want to avoid making political enemies, they must accommodate these demands and therefore steer a course between potentially conflicting interests of domestic groups. As a result, a response to WTO litigation involves these actors that stand to benefit or lose from compliance. Policymakers then cater to the requests made by the group that has more political clout when deciding to resist compliance with adverse panel rulings or to bring trade-liberalizing policy change.

In a world characterized by ever-increasing internationalization of production, I posit that the domestic balance of interests is much more conducive to the outcome of swift compliance when a dispute touches upon the interests of domestic actors—i.e., firms and sectors—that are highly integrated into value chains. The inclusion of these actors in the domestic political setting increases the political weight of the pro-trade group that prefers trade liberalization. This argument, however, bears similarities with earlier works in the field that need to be noted.

2.1.1 What Has Been Said About WTO Members Behavior at the DSM?

The literature on the WTO has come to examine a large array of issues, such as the extent to which WTO and its DSM contain protectionist responses to economic crises (Baccini and Kim 2012; Davis and Pelc 2015), the determinants of dispute initiation at the DSM (e.g., Busch et al. 2009; Davis 2012; Sattler and Bernauer 2011), why disputes escalate from consultation to the panel stage (e.g., Busch and Reinhardt 2006; Guzman and Simmons 2002; Busch 2000), whether or not dispute resolution actually increases trade between WTO Members (e.g., Bechtel and Sattler 2015; Chaudoin et al. 2016), reasons behind the judicial economy exercised by the dispute settlement panels (e.g., Busch and Pelc 2010), the domestic political implications of litigation on interest groups (e.g., Goldstein and Martin 2000), and the conditions under which WTO Members comply with their trade liberalization commitments at the WTO (e.g., Bown 2004).

In this literature, three main hypotheses have been proposed regarding WTO Members' behavior in response to international litigation. The first set of authors put forward that WTO Members avoid reneging on their commitments because of the threat of retaliation imposed upon them (e.g., Zangl 2008; Bown 2004; Mavroidis 2012).[2] According to this logic, members are more likely to uphold their trade-liberalizing commitments, especially when the dispute settlement panels request them to bring their policies in line with WTO rules, because the complainant members can credibly threaten the defendants with retaliation.

Secondly, authors who work in the field of international law have proposed that WTO Members are more likely to comply with adverse panel rulings when targeted policies required executive changes, rather than legislative changes (Wilson 2007; Brewster and Chilton 2014). The argument is that policies that need to be corrected (or withdrawn) by legislatures—e.g., the US Congress—than it takes WTO Members more time to change their policies because of administrative delays and the diverging interests of individuals in legislatures who might block proceedings. In line with this argument, some also put forward that the number of veto players whose consent is necessary to make domestic policy changes is a determinant of the ability of WTO Members to comply with WTO panel rulings (Young 2010; Poletti and De Bièvre 2014).

Thirdly, and lastly, a number of scholars have posited that WTO Members are more likely to comply with the rulings of the DSM when policymakers do not face protectionist demands from their domestic constituencies (Spilker 2012; Poletti and De Bièvre 2014). According to this argument, sectors that mobilize and press their protectionist preferences prevent WTO Members to bring forth compliance. When complainants target WTO-illegal policies, the ultimate change of policy depends on the support of the domestic actors that are affected by it in the defendants' economy. Therefore, when a dispute touches

[2] Bernhardt Zangl in his 2008 article also highlights reputational concerns and normative commitment to international law as reasons why WTO Members uphold their promises at the WTO DSM relative to dispute settlement under GATT. Yet, the author admits that the primary difference between the dispute settlement mechanisms of GATT and WTO are the powers given to the WTO to impose authorized retaliation, which he argues changed the behavior of the US in a number of disputes.

upon the interests of protectionist actors—e.g., producers of agricultural products—they mobilize and press their government to resist policy changes.

I share these assumptions about the nature of trade policymaking and consider the interests of domestic actors to be key in explaining trade policy outcome in response to WTO disputes. However, I go beyond these analyses in three ways and address the following shortcomings of this literature.

Firstly, and most importantly, these works do not account for the dispute settlement behavior WTO Members in the majority of disputes they are involved in. The proposed explanations cannot explain why the behavior of powerful WTO Members varies dramatically across the disputes they have with smaller economies, even sometimes against the same WTO Member (e.g., in the cases of the US disputes with Thailand). Similarly, current works fail to address how and why small WTO Members show variance in their behavior against powerful WTO Members with high retaliatory capacity (e.g., India's response to legal challenges by the US and Argentina's responses to litigation by the EU). The arguments that focus on the role of domestic trade-related interests also fail to account for the compliant behavior of the governments in disputes in which there was significant mobilized opposition to policy change (e.g., US' behavior in the steel safeguards dispute lodged by the EU). In other words, WTO Members sometimes comply very quickly with the rulings of the WTO panels despite mobilized domestic protectionist interests that seek to delay implementation.

Second, despite their quality, these works shed light on only a small part of the empirically-observable patterns of WTO Member behavior. Empirical research on WTO disputes focuses almost exclusively on certain WTO Members (Brewster and Chilton 2014; Wilson 2007; Young 2010), specific to certain sectors, (Spilker 2012) and rely on case studies (Poletti and De Bièvre 2014; Zangl 2008). Therefore, these important works can only offer limited generalizability regarding their findings. Moreover, these works do show with great clarity that the overwhelming majority of WTO dispute settlement cases involve democratic defendants with large administrative and legal capacity confronting complainants with credible retaliatory capacity (Horn et al. 2011). This means that we need to focus more on the behavior of WTO Members across the disputes they are involved in—rather than examining their behavior against other members.

I address these shortcomings and examine all of the WTO Members' responses to litigation and sketch out their behavior across the disputes they are involved in. In doing so, I test all of the aforementioned factors together and provide a more comprehensive picture of their relative explanatory power, rather than focusing on one or two factors that has an impact on WTO Members' behavior.[3]

Most importantly, however, my theoretical contribution comes from considering how the growing relevance of value chains in the contemporary international economy affects the political economy of trade and, ultimately, WTO Members' compliance with panel rulings. The literature has so far ignored the role of value chains in forming the preferences of domestic interests in response to WTO litigation and therefore faces an omitted variable bias. By disregarding the nature and the consequences of internationalization of production and integration into value chains, the analyses are missing an important piece of the puzzle that has the potential to explain how domestic interests are formed and under which conditions policymakers respond to WTO litigation with trade-liberalizing policy change.

2.2 The Argument: Value Chains, Firms, and Compliance

Value chains refer to a "full range of activities that firms engage into bring a product to the market, from conception to final use" (OECD 2013, p. 8). In a sense the title "chain" helps us understand and explain the fragmented nature of international trade and the growth of international ties among world economies. While the global rise in international economic ties is not a new phenomenon whatsoever (Smith 1776; Bentham 1800; Hellenier 1977), many would agree that world economies are becoming *ever more* deeply integrated (Sturgeon and Memedovic 2010). There is an exponentially growing body of research that analyzes the causes and consequences of the expansion of value chains that have structural implications for the global trade order (e.g., Gereffi 1994, 1999; Humphrey

[3] Clearly this is also due to the methodological homogeneity in the literature; a research design with case studies can only accommodate a few factors to be included in an analysis. Instead, a large-n approach *with* case studies would be more revealing. I have come to understand that the excruciatingly demanding data collection required for a large-n study of WTO Member behavior was an important reason why scholars limited their analyses.

and Schmitz 2002; Dossani and Kenney 2003; Dean et al. 2007; Escaith et al. 2010; Cattaneo et al. 2010). When firms engage in production across different countries, a range of other firms and their domestic economies are also involved in this complex network of economic activity. In turn, firms' linkages with other enterprises increase the expansion of value chains even further as current advancements in logistics and information technology make it easier to outsource (entire or parts of) productions into strategically desirable locales.

This internationalization of production has been empirically shown to be spreading both in developing and developed economies and tend to generate potentially positive impact on those firms' productivity, profits, and wage levels (Bernard et al. 2006; Miroudot et al. 2009; Goldberg et al. 2010). Yet, the precise measurement of value chain activities is faced with numerous problems, including but not limited to lack of generally-agreed characterization of "integration" and a lack of micro-data (Sturgeon and Gereffi 2010).

That being said, we can empirically observe that the rise of these networks results in at least two systematic changes for the global trade order; substantial increase in trade in parts and components, and the development of firms' affiliate ties with other enterprises. For one, trade in intermediate goods and services has taken a central point in global commercial activity. Today trade in intermediates accounts for over two thirds of total imports for the majority of OECD members (Johnson and Noguera 2012) and for about 90% of exports of US parents in manufacturing to affiliates abroad (Ramondo et al. 2011; see Miroudot et al. 2009 for data until 2006). Second, the continued rise in mergers and acquisitions has reached an unprecedented level, creates more and more linkages across (and within) firms. The increasing relevance of production networks in the world economy further indicates that international trade flows are largely shaped by patterns of economic integration centered around multinational corporations (MNCs).[4] Indeed, it has been reported that MNCs mediate more than 80% of US exports and imports (Bernard et al. 2009; Jensen et al. 2015).

These figures also suggest that policymakers will have strong incentives to cater to the demands of international firms to tackle trade barriers.

[4] See Institute for Mergers and Acquisitions for the number and value of M&A transactions worldwide since the 1980s—Accessible via: https://imaa-institute.org/mergers-and-acquisitions-statistics/.

This is so not only because they clearly have obvious stakes in eliminating trade barriers due to their extensive engagement in value chain activities. Perhaps most importantly, firms that operate within production networks also have greater capacity to mobilize politically and exercise political clout. These firms dispose of resources and face few collective action problems. For instance, only 1% of US firms both import and export (Bernard et al. 2009), and yet MNCs account for a sizable share of economic activity in the US, representing more than 27% of employment in 2000 and accounting for more than one-third of net job creation in the private sector from 1993 to 2000 (Jensen et al. 2015). In short, not only international firms have huge stakes in the elimination of trade barriers, they also have a large capacity to overcome collective action problems to mobilize and weigh in the policymaking process.

2.2.1 *Firms in Trade Policymaking*

What are the implications of internationalization of production on the politics of WTO dispute settlement? I develop an argument in this section that relies on two important assumptions about the nature of trade policymaking. Firstly, I assume that WTO Members generally aim to abide by their international trade commitments. This assumption stems from the largely accepted view that international law is mostly complied with, especially international trade law under the auspice of the WTO (Henkin 1979; Chayes and Chayes 1993; Eckhardt and Elsig 2015). WTO Members want to avoid incurring reputational costs and do not benefit from disrupting a system based on reciprocity (Tomz 2007; Fearon 1994; Keohane 1984; Axelrod 1984). Therefore, I expect policymakers to be in favor of keeping their trade-liberalizing commitments in place as a default position unless they face a compelling reason why they should resist complying—e.g., when protectionist interests mobilize in favor of non-compliance following WTO litigation.

Secondly, I assume governments implement trade policy based on the preferences of economic actors, which is a rather accepted view in the political economy literature (Grossman and Helpman 1994; Manger 2012; Shaffer 2003). Governments try to maximize support of economic actors for at least two reasons. First, they rely on the political support of their constituencies and avoid making political enemies. Therefore, they cater to the demands of domestic groups by responding to pressure (lobbying) stemming from them. In addition, governments have a structural incentive to support domestic interests by increasing economic activity and employment (Hiscox 2001; Milner 1987).

I accordingly consider firms to be political actors that press their preferences and influence policy outcomes, either by lobbying independently or through sector associations. I follow a number of recent works that attempt to examine firms as individual actors in trade policymaking (Jensen et al. 2015; Antràs and Helpman 2004; Helpman et al. 2004; Osgood 2016; Baccini et al. 2018). This literature primarily advances the seminal work of Melitz (2003) in highlighting sectors' product differentiation and firms' heterogeneous productivity to explain international trade patterns. Although the scientific progress made under this "new new trade theory" is not the focus of the theoretical development in this study, there are several important overlaps between the two. For one, this literature has pointed out that besides having trade-liberalizing preferences, the firms integrated into value chains prioritize lobbying in favor of strong investment clauses in PTAs to secure smooth trade flows across various countries along a value chain (Kim et al. 2019). My argument is consistent with this argument and extends this framework beyond PTAs and into compliance with existing rules—*in casu* the WTO agreements. I too argue firms want to avoid disruptions to their value chains, and when these disruptive trade policies are challenged at the WTO, they mobilize and demand the removal of such measures. Second, scholars working in this tradition have convincingly demonstrated that highly productive firms who engage in export are more likely to benefit from trade liberalization and they are the biggest supporters of trade liberalization and PTAs (Baccini et al. 2017; Osgood 2016, p. 25). The implications of exporters' support for trade liberalization are both relevant and crucial for my argument. Exporters who seek market access opportunities by supporting PTAs would equally be likely to support compliance at the WTO due to a potential threat of retaliation via market closures (Bown 2004). Therefore, the pro-compliance preferences of exporters add to the political weight of firms highly integrated into value chains who also wish to lower trade barriers—creating a domestic coalition in favor of faster compliance (Eckhardt and Poletti 2016; Yildirim 2017; Yildirim et al. 2018).

Moreover, in line with the literature I also consider these international firms as capable of mobilizing with relative ease—reiterating the point I made in the previous section. Firstly, international firms that are integrated into value chains tend to be the most productive and profitable ones (Helpman et al. 2004), which means they have the financial resources to undertake comprehensive lobbying activities. Secondly, these firms face fewer collective action problems, as they tend to operate in specialized markets with high concentration (Kim 2012). In addition, for firms in differentiated markets, political activity may be undertaken by single firms acting on their own with the support of affiliates, subsidiaries, and arm's length suppliers (e.g., Lanz and Miroudot 2011; Jensen et al. 2013) or, alternatively, the interests of firms may align for particular products used as inputs in production processes, and in those instances they would get into a coalition with other importers asking for the removal of the challenged trade barriers (e.g., Gilligan 1997).

Accordingly, I consider highly international firms to be represented by sector associations who translate firms' aggregate collective preferences to policymakers. In other words, a sector that is highly integrated into value chains basically refers to a sector that is populated (at least in majority or more) by highly international firms that are integrated into production networks via different means. I recognize that firm-level lobbying studies have shown how firms conduct independent political activity, and while that may very well be, I operate here with the assumption that for the purposes of WTO litigation, firms are much more likely to operate politically through sectors. This is because WTO disputes often involve a range of products in a given sector, rather than a single product that might affect a particular firm. In turn, firms whose interests are aligned are likely to enter into a coalition in the context of international litigation and press for their preferences together. Moreover, as I noted above dispute settlement proceedings are extremely costly and public–private partnerships involve significant resources that need to be marshaled. Therefore, firms' political activity in WTO dispute settlement through sectors is much more common that makes it easier to mobilize resources and subsequently increases the political clout of firms.

2.2.2 *Integration into Value Chains and Firms' Preferences*

In general, the above-mentioned literature showed that integration into value chains increases demands for lower trade barriers in order for firms to enjoy value-added trade (Jensen et al. 2013). As firms now (more than ever) use foreign affiliates, subsidiaries, and arm's length suppliers in their production processes, they slowly create a "factory world" (Los et al. 2014). Their activities across borders have been demonstrated to promote and deepen Preferential Trade Agreements (PTAs). Yet, even though many works have examined the effect of domestic economic actors' value chain integration in a bilateral setting, these analyses have ignored the multilateral setting of the WTO (Antràs and Staiger 2012; Baccini et al. 2018; Kim 2015; Orefice and Rocha 2014). Accordingly, I examine the potential impact of these networks at the multilateral level and analyze the extent to which firms' policy preferences and their aggregated demands through sectors impact WTO Members' behavior at the dispute settlement mechanism.

I focus on two characteristics of firms in order to grasp their integration into value chains; their involvement in the processing of intermediates and their association with foreign enterprises—I outline them in Fig. 2.1. Numerous studies in the field of international political economy have established that trade in intermediate goods and services and outsourcing are the most straightforward measure of value chain integration (Eckhardt and Poletti 2016; Amador and Cabral 2014, p. 19; Bernard and Jensen 1995). Thus, I take into account these two properties of firms and

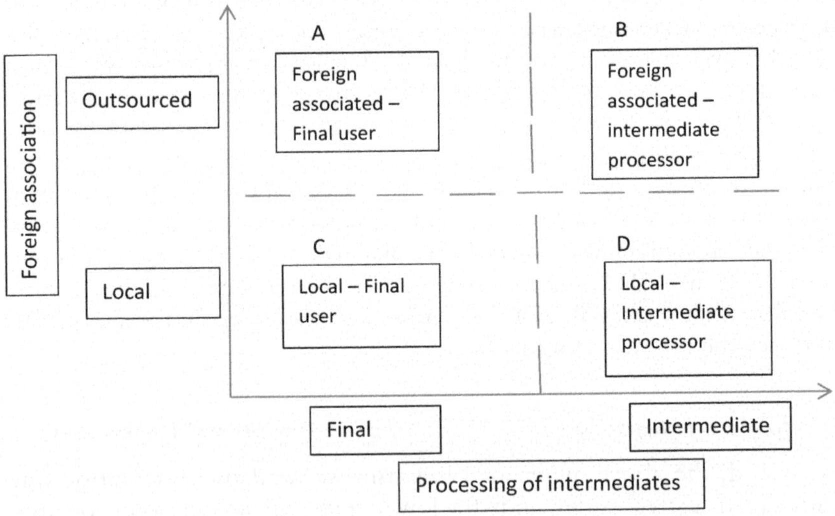

Fig. 2.1 Two characteristics of firms' (and sectors') value chain integration (*Source* Author)

sectors to define their level of integration into value chains. Moreover, I consider four types of firms that operate in an economy, which are shown collectively in Fig. 2.2. Each of these types has variation along the two properties I noted above and their expected trade policy preferences are outlined in the following page.

Type 1: Import-competing firms that operate only in the domestic economy. These firms engage in minimal, if at all, trade with foreign enterprises and they may be processing intermediate products, if they are suppliers of inputs. They are split into two subgroups; manufacturing import-competitors and non-manufacturers. In cases where firms in this category are producing goods and services, they may act as the lowest

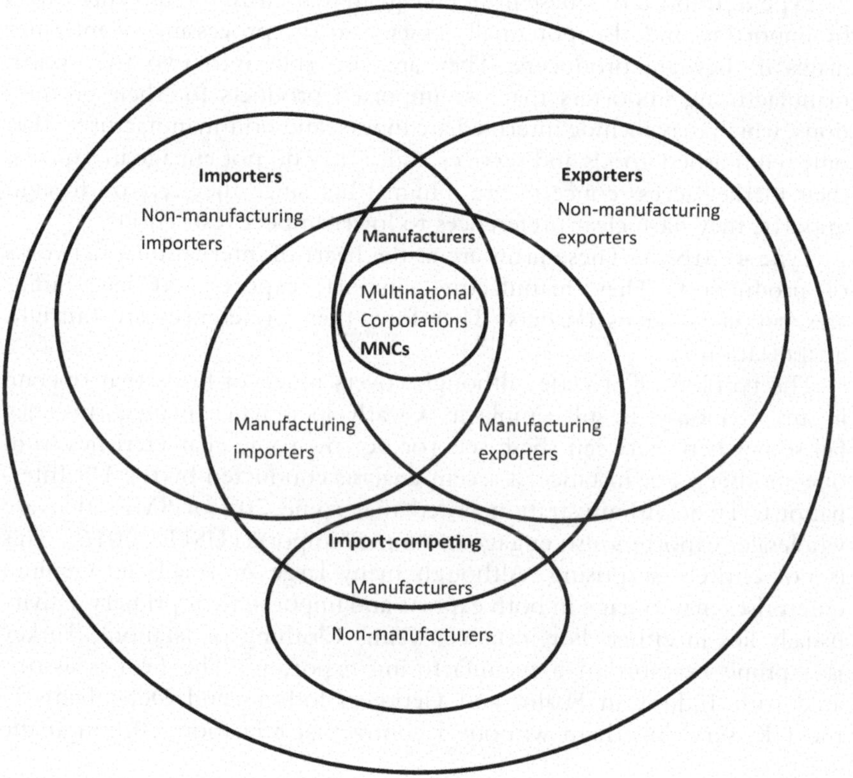

Fig. 2.2 A typology of firms (*Source* Author)

part of a chain and provide (domestically made) inputs to be processed. In cases where they do not produce, they engage in retail sales. In either case, however, they prefer protective trade barriers in order to avoid competition from imported products.

Type 2: Exporters. These firms engage in trade with foreign enterprises and also potentially engage in intermediate trade—although this is not assumed across the board. These firms are split into two subgroups as well, manufacturers that produce goods and services and non-manufacturers that are wholesalers and suppliers. Regardless of their production capacity, however, they have clear-cut market access preferences to export their products and thus prefer low market access barriers.

Type 3: Importers. These firms engage in trade with foreign enterprises by importing and also potentially engage in the processing of intermediates if they are producers. They are also split into two subgroups, manufacturing importers that use imported products for their productions, which may include intermediate inputs, and non-manufacturers that only sell finished goods and services. Since they do not engage in exports, their market access concerns are minimal but since they rely on foreign imports, they have clear preferences to lower import restrictions.

Type 4: MNCs. These firms are at the heart of international networks of production. They manufacture, import, export, and have affiliates/suppliers across borders. Therefore, their preferences are outright liberalization.

The typology I provide, although covers much of firms that operate in any economy, is still simplistic. Clearly in practice many firms may fall somewhere between these sets (or borrow some characteristics from one another). For instance, a recent analysis conducted by the US International Trade Administration noted that some 70% of SMEs that are wholesaler exporters also engage in "some" imports (USITA 2016). This is not entirely surprising. Although many large or small-and-medium enterprises may engage in both exports and imports, their primary activity usually lies in either. For instance, Venus Clothing of Istanbul, Turkey is a prime example of a manufacturing exporter.[5] The firm is associated with Inditex in Spain, and George Clothing and Debenhams in the UK, servicing them without a contractual affiliation. Although the

[5] For additional information, see: http://www.venusgiyim.com.tr/en/index.html.

Table 2.1 General trade policy preferences of above-described firms

Type of firm		*General trade policy preference*
1. Import competing		Protection
2. Exporter	a. Manufacturer	Market access
	b. Non-manufacturer	Market access
3. Importer	c. Manufacturer	Low import barriers
	d. Non-manufacturer	Low import barriers
4. MNCs		Both market access and low import barriers

production plant of the firm engages in exports of finished textiles to overseas markets, they also import some basic raw materials from overseas, such as cotton from India, to produce a final product, e.g., Zara T-shirt. The plant of some 300 people primarily serves as a manufacturing exporter under my typology. However, it still engages in imports, albeit as a minimal part of its operation.

I therefore presume that a large part of firms' operation would still fall under one on of the above-described classifications. In Table 2.1, I outline these firms' general trade policy preferences before I move on to the implications of their preferences regarding compliance with WTO rulings.

2.2.3 *WTO Dispute Settlement System in Brief*

This general characterization at hand, I will now turn to my expectations regarding firms' responses to WTO litigation after I briefly introduce the WTO dispute settlement system, which is a legal system that unfolds in several discrete steps. The process begins when one or more members of the WTO file a formal complaint and request consultations on specific trade policy measures taken by another member. Consultations take place as confidential negotiations between the parties. If they fail to solve the issue at this stage, the complainant can request the Dispute Settlement Body establish a panel of experts. The panel members then prepare an interim report, about which the parties can negotiate during the process of writing. At this stage, the parties are encouraged to reach a mutually agreed upon solution. If they do not, the panel circulates its ruling in the form of an initial report (WTO 2004). Both parties may accept the ruling, in which case the dispute would end. However, the respondent and the complainant also have a chance to appeal to the ruling. If they do so, the dispute reaches the appeals phase, where the standing Appellate Body (AB) reviews the dispute. The AB then issues a final ruling on the dispute, in which it may overturn or uphold the panel ruling in part or in its entirety. In disputes where the AB sides with some or all of the accusations of the complainant, the dispute moves to the implementation phase. At this stage, the respondent party is asked "to bring the measures into conformity" with WTO law and is asked to notify the DSB of its implementation. In case of enduring non-compliance, the DSB can authorize the complainant to put in place retaliatory measures against the defendant.

Two features of the DSM are crucial to understand the political-economic dynamics that underlie its functioning. First, WTO Members are the only enforcers of WTO contracts. While governmental representatives crucially depend on information provided by private industry, they are the only ones who can trigger WTO adjudication, not the Secretariat of the WTO in the role of a supranational prosecutor, nor private actors (Hoekman and Mavroidis 2000).[6] Second, the DSM remains largely a bilateral and decentralized enforcement mechanism, as the ultimate remedy in enduring cases of non-compliance with a WTO ruling comes in the form of retaliation by the complainant.

2.2.4 *Containing Protectionist Interests and Overcoming Resistance to Compliance*

In the context of WTO dispute settlement, my argument highlights the importance of importers—i.e., Type 3 firms. These actors have very clear preferences to avoid imposition of import barriers in their domestic economies. Moreover, they face very stark distributional consequences in response to a higher import duty or a limit on imports. Therefore, the certainty of losses is likely to incentivize them to mobilize.

Consider the behavior of US firms in response to heightening trade tensions between the US and its partners. After President Trump announced his plan to introduce a so-called border adjustment tax in late 2016, American importers mobilized very quickly and (at least

[6] On the private–public partnership in WTO dispute settlement, see Shaffer (2003).

temporarily) delayed the imposition of this particular trade barrier. Following the raising of tariff duties on steel and aluminum products, highly integrated companies again lobbied for the removal of the duties, using domestic litigation to halt it. Regardless of them achieving their policy objectives, however, the point here is to show the stark distributional consequences of trade restrictions on the cost of their operations, which in turn incentivizes them to mobilize politically. These firms face very stark distributional consequences of trade barriers because a barrier that raises customs duties of a product, or limits the number of the products that can enter a market increases the operating cost of firms and accordingly lowers their profits.

When a dispute is launched at the WTO, 90% of the time it targets a policy that restricts exports into a WTO Member's economy (Bown and Reynolds 2014, p. 8). We expect in this scenario that litigant member would push for the opening of markets, and the defendant member has the option to remove the trade barrier or resist compliance. From a defendant's perspective, the economic actors (who are being protected by the challenged measure in the first place) will mobilize to keep them in place. On the contrary, exporters are expected to mobilize in favor of removing the measures as fast as possible since they fear retaliation in the form of market closures.

This scenario highlights the existing studies' focus on two sets of domestic interests: import-competitors and exporters.[7] Under these circumstances, the politics of compliance is seen as a battle between import competitors who lobby their government representatives to keep the import-restricting policy in place, to protect themselves from foreign competitors in the domestic market (Bown 2004), and exporters who mobilize to ask for compliance to avoid the imposition of retaliatory measures, which may harm their access to the complainant's market. This scenario is outlined in Fig. 2.3.

Policymakers in this scenario face considerable resistance to compliance because the status quo protects the anti-compliance group that seeks prolonged protection. Yet, policymakers are able to overcome this resistance if a dispute involves firms that rely on imports. With the involvement of importers the weight of pro-compliance constituencies in a defendant WTO Member essentially increases. Moreover, for those firms

[7] This is assuming that factors of production are not perfectly mobile across sectors (Hiscox 2001).

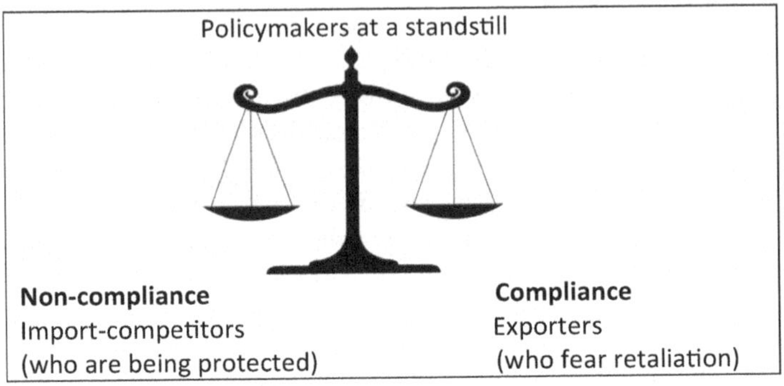

Fig. 2.3 Policymakers face resistance to comply (*Source* Author)

that use imports to produce as well as export goods and services, the removal of the trade barrier is preferred both because they face potential market access restrictions ***and*** because imports are more expensive. The domestic constellation of interests in this scenario is outlined on Table 2.2.

In such a scenario, policymakers encounter a different dynamic of domestic political actors, one which also includes importers (and potentially MNCs), which shifts the balance of interests in favor of a stronger pro-compliance coalition. It is crucial here to reiterate a small remark made above though; about 90% of disputes target a policy that restricts exports into WTO Member's economy (Bown and Reynolds 2014, p. 8). This means that disputes disproportionately affect importing firms. Therefore, I am more interested in MNCs that also import to mobilize. Readers might wonder where MNCs play a role here, and it must be stated explicitly that the term "importer" here does not directly exclude MNCs. Quite

Table 2.2 Trade policy preferences of firms in response to WTO litigation

Type of firm	*General trade policy preference*	*Policy preference in response to litigation*
1. Import competing	Protection	Continued protection
2. Exporters	Liberalization	Compliance
3. Importers	Liberalization	Compliance

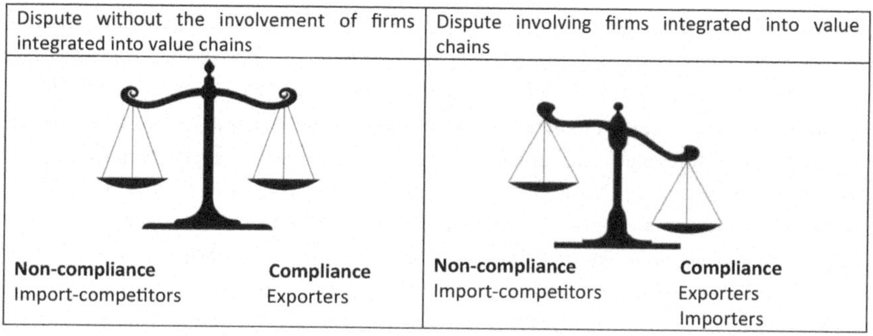

Fig. 2.4 Change in domestic constellation of interests in disputes involving firms integrated into value chains (*Source* Author)

the opposite, as my typology suggests, there are MNCs that also import, which are quite likely to mobilize when their interests are threatened.

If and when a dispute involves firms integrated into value chains that primarily leads them to rely on imports, a change in the domestic balance of interests can be expected—this is visualized on Fig. 2.4.

With import-dependent firms pressing their pro-compliance preferences, the domestic costs of non-compliance are much higher for policy-makers, and therefore, the defendant WTO Members are able to contain protectionist interests faster. This leads to the following hypothesis:

The higher the affected firms' degree of integration into value chains, the faster the compliance.

It is important to note that the logic of my argument should not depend significantly on whether trade in intermediates is characterized by high or low levels of intra-industry trade (IIT). IIT trade is a result of product differentiation motivated both by economies of scale and consumers' taste for variety (Krugman 1981). Baccini et al. (2018) argue that support for trade liberalization should be high in the presence of low levels of IIT in trade in intermediates, while it should decrease with increasing levels of IIT. The authors argue that low levels of IIT mean that intermediates are relatively homogeneous and can therefore be equally used by all domestic import-dependent firms, while high levels of IIT mean that intermediates are more differentiated, making it difficult for domestic downstream sectors to switch to new varieties of intermediates, and ultimately decreasing political support for trade liberalization among import-dependent firms. However, while it may be true that support for trade liberalization should decrease, opposition to it is also likely to decrease. Precisely because high levels of IIT means high levels of product specialization and strong buyer-relationships between domestic producers of intermediates, downstream sectors, and consumers, domestic import-dependent firms that cannot enjoy the benefits of cheaper access to intermediates should not be particularly worried about being driven out of business. In other words, while trade in intermediates due to high levels of value chain integration varies significantly depending on levels of IIT, I do not expect this variation to affect in significant ways the likelihood of compliance in WTO disputes.

2.2.5 *Why Do Trade Barriers Get Erected in the First Place?*

Instinctively, we can understand why firms mobilize once there is a trade dispute that involves them. However, this does not explain why they cannot prevent the erection of trade barriers in the first place. If highly mobilized, politically influential firms are hurt by a trade barrier; must they not have prevented such barriers to be raised? The answer is not necessarily. The reasoning behind is quite straightforward and depends on the relative political power that lies in the coalition of pro-trade group(s) in a domestic economy. In the absence of a trade barrier (and a dispute) the pro-trade constituency in a domestic economy is much smaller than after the erection of a trade barrier that is targeted in a dispute. While domestic pro-trade groups may not necessarily sway the opinion policy-makers, due to their smaller sizes, their coalition grows with the addition of exporters that mobilize due to threat of retaliation a dispute brings about. In essence, therefore, trade barriers need not necessarily be tackled by pro-trade advocates before they are erected. Once they are raised and targeted in a WTO dispute, however, the size and the political clout of the pro-trade group increases and it is more likely that they are tackled at that stage.

2.3 The Empirical Approach

In order to test the theoretical expectation I posited above, i.e., disputes involving firms that are highly integrated into value chains will result in faster compliance, I combine a statistical examination involving Cox survival analysis with in-depth case studies. By combining quantitative and qualitative research methods, I aim to be methodologically eclectic in order to investigate my phenomenon with the most appropriate and useful techniques available. To explain *patterns* of WTO Member behavior across the disputes they are involved in, I examine each and every dispute that resulted in a panel ruling, and thus investigate the full universe of cases, which is the aim of the first part of the empirical section using Cox proportional hazard modeling, a type of regression technique that involves survival analysis to look at the factors that impact *how long* a unit of observation survives given confounding factors' impact (Fox and Weisberg 2011). Since I am interested in the *time* it takes for WTO Members to bring compliance following panel rulings, this method uniquely allows me to see the impact of factors on the "death" of a dispute by taking into account a number of potential confounding factors operationalized as quantitative variables.

However, by using more aggregate measures without micro-data involving firm' trade across value chains and firms' political activity, my large-n demonstration is limited in what it can offer. In order to (partially) remedy this shortcoming, I employ case studies to understand *how* firms' political mobilization shorten or lengthen the compliance process of WTO Member governments, examining detailed analysis of firms' coalition building and their political activity. In-depth case studies allow me to not only test my theory but also to demonstrate the causal mechanism I have postulated. In order to do that, I use process tracing and show how firms mobilize and press their trade policy preferences in response to disputes. Drawing on my large-n analysis, I identify cases in which a particular constellation of interests can be observed. I then examine these cases comparatively using firm-level data—including lobbying spending and firm affiliate data—and be able to demonstrate the impact of my theory with much more precision.

References

Amador, João, and S. Cabral. 2014. Global Value Chains Surveying Drivers and Measures. Working Paper 1739 (2014). European Central Bank (ECB), Frankfurt. Available at https://www.ecb.europa.eu/pub/pdf/scpwps/ecbwp1739.en.pdf?13f6d86f40a3c60325f27cbc08a18742. Accessed on March 22, 2016.

Antràs, Pol, and Elhanan Helpman. 2004. Global Sourcing. *Journal of Political Economy* 112 (3): 552–580.

Antràs, Pol, and Robert W. Staiger. 2012. Offshoring and the Role of Trade Agreements. *American Economic Review* 102 (7): 3140–3183.

Axelrod, Robert. 1984. *The Evolution of Cooperation*. New York: Basic.

Axelrod, R., and R. Keohane. 1985. Achieving Cooperation Under Anarchy: Strategies and Institutions. *World Politics* 38 (1): 226–254.

Baccini, L., and S.Y. Kim. 2012. Preventing Protectionism: International Institutions and Trade Policy. *The Review of International Organizations* 7 (4): 369–398.

Baccini, L., A. Dür, and M. Elsig. 2018. Intra-Industry Trade, Global Value Chains, and the Political Economy of Preferential Trade Liberalization. *International Studies Quarterly* 62 (2): 329–340.

Baccini, Leonardo, Pablo M. Pinto, and Stephen Weymouth. 2017. The Distributional Consequences of Preferential Trade Liberalization: Firm-Level Evidence. *International Organization* 71 (2): 373–95.

Barrett, S. 2007. *Why Cooperate? The Incentive to Supply Global Public Goods*. Oxford: Oxford University Press (Oxford Scholarship Online).

Bentham, J. 1800. The Manual of Political Economy. In *The Collected Works of Jeremy Bentham*, ed. Michael Quinn. Oxford: Oxford University Press.

Bernard, A., and B. Jensen. 1995. Exporters, Jobs, and Wages in U.S. Manufacturing: 1976–1987. Brookings Papers on Economic Activity, Microeconomics, 67–119.

Bernard, A., B. Jensen, and P.K. Schott. 2006. Survival of the Best Fit: Exposure to Low-Wage Countries and the (Uneven) Growth of U.S. Manufacturing Plants. *Journal of International Economics* 68 (1): 219–237.

Bernard, A., B. Jensen, and P.K. Schott. 2009. Importers, Exporters, and Multinationals: A Portrait of Firms in the U.S. That Trade Goods. In *Producer Dynamics*, ed. Timothy Dunne, J. Bradford Jensen, and Mark J. Roberts. Chicago: University of Chicago Press.

Bernhagen, P. 2008. Business and International Environmental Agreements: Domestic Sources of Participation and Compliance by Advanced Industrialized Democracies. *Global Environmental Politics* 8 (1): 78–110.

Bown, C. 2004. On the Economic Success of GATT/WTO Dispute Settlement. *The Review of Economics and Statistics* 86 (3): 811–823.

Bown, C. 2009. *Self-Enforcing Trade: Developing Countries and WTO Dispute Settlement*. Washington: Brookings Institution Press.

Bown, C., and K. Reynolds. 2014. Trade Flows and Trade Disputes. Policy Research Working Paper 6979. Development Research Team, World Bank, Washington.

Brewster, R. 2012. Reputation in International Relations and International Law Theory. In *Interdisciplinary Perspectives on International Law and International Relations—The State of the Art*, ed. Jeffrey Dunoff and Mark Pollack. Cambridge: Cambridge University Press.

Brewster, R., and A. Chilton. 2014. Supplying Compliance: Why and When the United States Complies with WTO Rulings. *Yale Journal of International Law* 39 (2): 201–247.

Busch, M. 2000. Bargaining in the Shadow of the Law: Early Settlement in GATT/WTO Disputes. *Fordham International Law Journal* 24: 158–172.

Busch, M., and K. Pelc. 2010. The Politics of Judicial Economy at the World Trade Organization. *International Organization* 64 (2): 257–259.

Bechtel, M., and T. Sattler. 2015. What Is Litigation in the World Trade Organization Worth? *International Organization* 69 (2): 375–403.

Busch, M., and E. Reinhardt. 2006. Three's a Crowd: Third Parties and WTO Dispute Settlement. *World Politics* 58 (3): 446–477.

Busch, M., E. Reinhardt, and G. Shaffer. 2009. Does Legal Capacity Matter? A Survey of WTO Members. *World Trade Review* 8 (4): 559–577.

Cattaneo, O., G. Gereffi, and C. Staritz. 2010. *Global Value Chains in a Postcrisis World: A Development Perspective*. Washington, DC: The World Bank. Available at http://issuu.com/world.bank.publications/docs/9780821384992. Accessed on May 22, 2017.

Chaudoin, S., J. Kucik, and K. Pelc. 2016. Do WTO Disputes Actually Increase Trade? *International Studies Quarterly* 0: 1–13. Advanced online publication. Available at http://isq.oxfordjournals.org/content/early/2016/04/15/isq.sqw009.

Chayes, A., and A.H. Chayes. 1993. On Compliance. *International Organization* 47 (2): 175–205.

Conti, J. 2010. *Between Law and Diplomacy: The Social Contexts of Disputing at the World Trade Organization*. Oxford: Oxford University Press.

Dai, X. 2005. Why Comply? The Domestic Constituency Mechanism. *International Organization* 59 (2): 363–398.

Dai, X. 2008. Effectiveness of International Environmental Institutions. *Global Environmental Politics* 8 (3): 154–158.

Davis, C. 2012. *Why Adjudicate: Enforcing Trade Rules in the WTO*. Princeton, NJ: Princeton University Press.

Davis, C., and K. Pelc. 2015. Cooperation in Hard Times: Self-Restraint of Trade Protection. *Journal of Conflict Resolution*. https://doi.org/10.1177/0022002715595699.

Dean, J.M., K.C. Fung, and Z. Wang. 2007. Measuring the Vertical Specialization in Chinese Trade. Working Paper, No. 2007-01-A. U.S. International Trade Commission, Office of Economics.

Dossani, R., and M. Kenney. 2003. Lift and Shift; Moving the Back Office to India. *Information Technologies and International Development* 1 (2): 21–37.

Dunoff, J., and M. Pollack. 2012. International Law and International Relations: Introducing an Interdisciplinary Dialogue. In *Interdisciplinary Perspectives on International Law and International Relations: The State of the Art*, ed. Jeffrey Dunoff and Mark Pollack. Cambridge: Cambridge University Press.

Eckhardt, J., and M. Elsig. 2015. Support for International Trade Law: The US and the EU Compared. *International Journal of Constitutional Law* 13 (4): 966–986.

Eckhardt, J., and A. Poletti. 2016. The Politics of Global Value Chains: Import Dependent Firms and EU-Asia Trade Agreements. *Journal of European Public Policy*. https://doi.org/10.1080/13501763.2015.1085073.

Escaith, H., L. Nannette, and S. Miroudot. 2010. International Supply Chains and Trade Elasticity in Times of Global Crisis. Economic Research and Statistics, World Trade Organization, January 30.

Fearon, J. 1994. Domestic Political Audiences and the Escalation of International Disputes. *The American Political Science Review* 88 (3): 577–592.

Fox, J., and S. Weisberg. 2011. *An R Companion to Applied Regression*, 2nd ed. Thousand Oaks, CA: Sage.

Gereffi, G. 1994. The Organization of Buyer-Driven Global Commodity Chains: How U.S. Retailers Shape Overseas Production Networks. In *Commodity Chains and Global Capitalism*, ed. G. Gereffi and M. Korzeniewicz, 95–122. Westport, CT: Praeger.

Gereffi, G. 1999. International Trade and Industrial Upgrading in the Apparel Commodity Chain. *Journal of International Economics* 48 (1): 37–70.

Gilligan, M. 1997. Lobbying as a Private Good with Intra-Industry Trade. *International Studies Quarterly* 41: 455–474.

Goldberg P., A. Khandelwal, N. Pavcnik, and P. Topalova. 2010. Imported Intermediate Inputs and Domestic Product Growth: Evidence from India. *The Quarterly Journal of Economics* 125 (4): 1727–1767.

Goldstein, Judith, and Lisa L. Martin. 2000. Legalization, Trade Liberalization, and Domestic Politics: A Cautionary Note. *International Organization* 54 (3): 603–632.

Grossman, G., and E. Helpman. 1994. Protection for Sale. *The American Economic Review* 84 (4): 833–850.

Guzman, A. 2008. *How International Law Works: A Rational Choice Theory*. Oxford: Oxford University Press.

Guzman, A., and B. Simmons. 2002. To Settle or Empanel? An Empirical Analysis of Litigation and Settlement at the WTO. *Journal of Legal Studies* 31 (1): 205–235.

Hafner-Burton, E. 2005. Trading Human Rights: How Preferential Trade Agreements Influence Government Repression. *International Organization* 59 (593): 629.

Hathaway O.A. 2002. Do Human Treaties Make a Difference? *The Yale Law Journal* 111 (8): 1935–2034.

Hellenier, G.K. 1977. Transnational Enterprises and the New Political Economy of U.S. Trade Policy. *Oxford Economic Papers* 29 (1): 102–116. Available at http://econpapers.repec.org/article/oupoxecpp/v_3a29_3ay_3a1977_3ai_3a1_3ap_3a102-16.htm. Accessed on March 3, 2017.

Helpman, E., M. Marc, and S. Yeaple. 2004. Export Versus FDI with Heterogeneous Firms. *The American Economic Review* 94 (1): 300–316.

Henkin, Louis. 1979. *How Nations Behave*. Washington: Council on Foreign Relations Publications.

Hiscox, M.J. 2001. Class Versus Industry Cleavages: Inter-Industry Factor Mobility and the Politics of Trade. *International Organization* 55: 1–46.

Hoekman, B., and P. Mavroidis. 2000. WTO Dispute Settlement, Transparency and Surveillance. *World Economy* 23 (4): 527–542.

Horn, H., L. Johannesson, and P. Mavroidis. 2011. The WTO Dispute Settlement System 1995–2010: Some Descriptive Statistics. *Journal of World Trade* 45 (6): 1107–1138.

Humphrey, J., and H. Schmitz. 2002. How Does Insertion in Global Value Chains Affect Upgrading in Industrial Clusters? *Regional Studies* 36 (9): 1017–1027.

Jensen, B., D. Quinn, and S. Weymouth. 2013. Global Supply Chains, Currency Undervaluation, and Firm Protectionist Demands. Working Paper 19239. National Bureau of Economic Research, Cambridge, MA. Available at http://www.nber.org/papers/w19239. Accessed on September 17, 2015.

Jensen, B., D. Quinn, and S. Weymouth. 2015. The Influence of Firm Global Supply Chains and Foreign Currency Undervaluations on US Trade Disputes. *International Organization* 69: 913–947.

Johnson, R.C., and G. Noguera. 2012. Accounting for Intermediates: Production Sharing and Trade in Value Added. *Journal of International Economics* 86 (2): 224–236.

Keohane, R. 1984. *After Hegemony: Cooperation and Discord in the World Political Economy*. Princeton, NJ: Princeton University Press.

Keohane, R., and J. Nye. 1977. *Power and Interdependence: World Politics in Transition*. New York: Brown University Press.

Kim, S.Y. 2012. Protectionism During Recession: Is This Time Different? *The Political Economist* 9 (2): 6–8.

Kim, S.Y. 2015. Regionalization in Search of Regionalism: Production Networks and Deep Integration Commitments in Asia's PTAs. In *The Purpose, Design, and Effects of Preferential Trade Agreements*, ed. Andreas Dür and Manfred Elsig. Cambridge: Cambridge University Press.

Kim, In Song, Helen V. Milner, Thomas Bernauer, Iain Osgood, Gabriele Spilker, and Dustin Tingley. 2019. Firms and Global Value Chains: Identifying Firms' Multidimensional Trade Preferences. *International Studies Quarterly* 63 (1): 153–167.

Koremenos, B. 2012. Institutionalism and International Law. In *Interdisciplinary Perspectives on International Law and International Relations—The State of the Art*, ed. Jeffrey Dunoff and Mark Pollack. Cambridge: Cambridge University Press.

Krasner, S.D. 1983. *International Regimes*. Ithaca, NY: Cornell University Press.

Krugman, P. 1981. Intraindustry Specialization and the Gains from Trade. *Journal of Political Economy* 89 (5): 959–973.

Lanz, Rainer, and Sébastien Miroudot. 2011. Intra-Firm Trade: Patterns, Determinants and Policy Implications. Working Paper 114. Trade Policy Papers. Organization for Economic Cooperation and Development (OECD) Publishing, Paris. Available at http://www.oecd-ilibrary.org/trade/intra-firm-trade_5kg9p39lrwnn-en. Accessed on April 12, 2016.

Los, Bart, Marcel P. Timmer, and Gaaitzen de Vries. 2014. How Global Are Global Value Chains? A New Approach to Measure International Fragmentation. *Journal of Regional Science* 55: 66–92.

Manger, Mark. 2012. Vertical Trade Specialization and the Formation of North-South PTAs. *World Politics* 64 (4): 622–658.

Mansfield, E., H. Milner, and Jon Pevehouse. 2007. Vetoing Co-operation: The Impact of Veto Players on Preferential Trading Agreements. *British Journal of Political Science* 37 (3): 403–432.

Martin, L. 2000. *Democratic Commitments: Legislatures and International Cooperation*. Princeton: Princeton University Press.

Mavroidis, Petros. 2012. On Compliance in the WTO: Enforcement Among Unequal Disputants. Briefing Paper No. 4. Geneva: CUTS International.

Melitz, Marc. 2003. The Impact of Trade on Intra-Industry Reallocations and Aggregate Industry Productivity. *Econometrica* 71 (6): 1695–1725.

Milner, H. 1987. Resisting the Protectionist Temptation: Industry and the Making of Trade Policy in France and the United States During the 1970s. *International Organization* 41 (4): 639–665.

Milner, H. 1997. *Interests, Institutions, and Information: Domestic Politics and International Relations*. Princeton: Princeton University Press.

Miroudot, S., R. Lanz, and A. Ragoussis. 2009. Trade in Intermediate Goods and Services. OECD Trade Policy Working Paper No. 93, November 3. Available at https://www.oecd.org/trade/its/44056524.pdf. Accessed on May 22, 2017.

Moravcsik, A. 2012. Liberal Theories of International Law, In *Interdisciplinary Perspectives on International Law and International Relations—The State of the Art*, ed. Jeffrey L. Dunoff and Mark A. Pollack. Cambridge: Cambridge University Press.

Morrow, J. 2007. When Do States Follow the Laws of War? *American Political Science Review* 101 (3): 559–572.

Organization for Economic Cooperation and Development (OECD). 2013. Interconnected Economies: Benefiting from Global Value Chains. Policy Synthesis Report. https://www.oecd.org/sti/ind/interconnected-economies-GVCs-synthesis.pdf. Accessed on February 11, 2017.

Orefice, G., and N. Rocha. 2014. Deep Integration and Production Networks: An Empirical Analysis. *The World Economy* 37 (1): 106–136.

Osgood, I. 2016. The Breakdown of Industrial Opposition to Trade: Firms, Product Variety and Reciprocal Liberalization. *World Politics*. https://doi.org/10.1017/S0043887116000174.

Poletti, A. 2017. Robert Keohane: The Promises of Cooperation. In *Classics in International Relations*, ed. Filippo Andreatta. Bologna: Il Mulino Publishing.

Poletti, A., and D. De Bièvre. 2014. Political Mobilization, Veto Players, and WTO Litigation: Explaining European Union Responses in Trade Disputes. *Journal of European Public Policy* 21 (8): 1181–1198.

Putnam, R. 1988. Diplomacy and Domestic Politics: The Logic of Two-Level Games. *International Organization* 42 (3): 427–460.

Ramondo, N., V. Rappoport, and K. Ruhl. 2011. Horizontal vs Vertical FDI: Revisiting Evidence from U.S. Multinationals, Working Paper. Available at https://ideas.repec.org/p/ste/nystbu/11-12.html. Accessed on May 22, 2017.

Sattler, T., and T. Bernauer. 2011. Gravitation or Discrimination? Determinants of litigation at the World Trade Organization. *European Journal of Political Research* 50 (2): 143–167.

Shaffer, G. 2003. *Defending Interests: Public-Private Partnerships in WTO Litigation*. Washington: Brookings Institution Press.

Simmons, B.A. 2000. International Law and State Behavior: Commitment and Compliance in International Monetary Affairs. *American Political Science Review* 94 (4): 819–835.

Simmons, B.A. 2009. *Mobilizing Human Rights: International Law in Domestic Politics*. Cambridge: Cambridge University Press.

Slaughter, A. 1995. International Law in a World of Liberal States. *European Journal of International Law* 6 (1): 503–538.

Smith, A. 1776. *An Inquiry into the Nature and Causes of the Wealth of Nations*. Edinburgh: William Strahan.

Snidal, D. 1985. Coordination Versus Prisoners' Dilemma: Implications for International Cooperation and Regimes. *American Political Science Review* 79 (4): 923–942.

Spilker, Gabriele. 2012. Compliance with WTO Dispute Rulings. Working Paper 2011–25. National Centre of Competence in Research Trade Regulation, Zurich, Switzerland.

Sturgeon, T., and G. Gereffi. 2010. Measuring Success in the Global Economy: Technological Learning, Industrial Upgrading, and Business Function Outsourcing in Global Value Chains. *Transnational Corporations* 17: 4. Available at https://unctad.org/en/docs/diaeiia200910a1_en.pdf. Accessed on June 20, 2020.

Sturgeon, T., and Olga Memedovic. 2010. Mapping Global Value Chains: Intermediate Goods Trade and Structural Change in the World Economy. United Nations Industrial Development Organization Working Paper 05/2010. Available at http://www.unido.org/fileadmin/media/documents/pdf/Publications/110905/WP052010_E.pdf. Accessed on April 29, 2017.

Tomz, M. 2007. Domestic Audience Costs in International Relations: An Experimental Approach. *International Organization* 61 (4): 821–840.

United States International Trade Administration (USITA). 2016. U.S. Export Fact Sheet—Export Statistics. Available at http://trade.gov/press/press-releases/2016/export-factsheet-040516.pdf. Accessed on February 2, 2017.

Von Stein, J. 2012. The Engines of Compliance. In *Synthesizing Insights from International Law and International Relations*, ed. Jeffrey Dunoff and Mark Pollack. Cambridge: Cambridge University Press.

Wilson, B. 2007. Compliance by WTO Members with Adverse WTO Dispute Settlement Rulings: The Record to Date. *Journal of International Economic Law* 10 (2): 397–403.

World Trade Organization. 2004. *Handbook on the WTO Dispute Settlement System*. Cambridge: Cambridge University Press.

Yildirim, Aydin. 2017. Domestic Political Implications of Global Value Chains: Explaining EU Responses to Litigation at the World Trade Organization. *Comparative European Politics*.

Yildirim, Aydin, Arlo Poletti, Tyson Chatagnier, and Dirk De Bievre. 2018. Internationalization of Production and Compliance in WTO Disputes. *Review of International Organizations* 13: 49–75.

Young, A.R. (2010). Effective Multilateralism on Trial: EU Compliance with WTO Law. In *The EU's Presence in International Organisations*, ed. S. Blavoukos and D. Bourantonis, vol. 67, 114–131. European Union Series: Routledge advances in European politics. Abingdon, UK: Routledge.

Zangl, Bernhard. 2008. Judicialization Matters! A Comparison of Dispute Settlement Under GATT and the WTO. *International Studies Quarterly* 52 (4): 825–854.

CHAPTER 3

Explaining Patterns of WTO Member Behavior at the WTO Dispute Settlement

Abstract Under what conditions do WTO Members change domestic policies or measures that are challenged in WTO litigation? This chapter tests the hypotheses put forward in the previous chapter and argues that the degree of integration into value chains of the economic sectors affected by a WTO dispute influences members' propensity to change domestic policies when targeted in WTO litigation. I propose that compliance with WTO rulings is faster when a domestic coalition consists of pro-trade liberalization groups composed of exporters seeking to avoid the imposition of retaliatory measures and import-dependent firms integrated into value chains wishing to exploit the opportunity to access cheaper imports. Under these circumstances, trade-liberalizing responses to WTO legal challenges are therefore more likely. I test this theory by relying on a novel database of WTO trade disputes and by estimating a Cox proportional hazard model. The results support my hypothesis and indicate that indeed when WTO-targeted measures involve sectors highly integrated into value chains, compliance with WTO panel rulings is faster.

Keywords Sectors · Value chain integration · Compliance · Cox regression

I start my empirical analysis by using a Cox proportional hazard model. In order to do so, I rely on a novel dataset of WTO trade disputes (which includes the EU as a single entity) that I have constructed over the last

A. B. Yildirim, *Value Chains and WTO Disputes*,
https://doi.org/10.1007/978-3-030-49094-2_3

few years. This dataset contains information on every WTO dispute that resulted in an adverse panel ruling between 1995 and 2016.[1] Although I recognize that recently-litigated disputes may bring additional variation to my analysis, I have reliable data only through 2016. As a result, my dataset includes 136 observations, after dropping cases with missing values. I use these data to examine the effect of value chain integration on the time it takes for defendants to implement WTO panels' recommendations. In addition to my variable of interest, I control for a number of relevant factors, drawn from the literature, which I outline below.

I measure my dependent variable, *time until compliance*, by calculating the number of months that it took defendants to implement adverse panel rulings. The universe of cases I consider is thus the set of WTO disputes in which a Panel or the Appellate Body issued an explicit and legally-binding injunction for the defendant to bring domestic policies into compliance with WTO rules. In doing so, I largely follow those works defining compliance as domestic policy change (Hudec 1993; Davey 2005; Busch and Reinhardt 2003) and complement this with taking into account how long it took violators to change their domestic policies (Brewster and Chilton 2014; Spilker 2012; Sattler et al. 2014). Because I both assume that politicians are primarily interested in obtaining support from politically relevant constituencies to enhance their chances of being re-elected or re-appointed (De Bièvre and Dür 2005; Olson 1965; Grossman and Helpman 2001) and are interested in gauging the effects of the dynamics of political mobilization of trade-related organized interests on the politics of compliance in WTO disputes, I believe this measure effectively allows me to capture the logic that underlies my argument. Indeed, variation in the extent to which governments swiftly correct their illegal behavior or rather use delay tactics and act as suppliers of such protectionist policies in the form of prolonged violations of WTO obligations at the WTO DSM can be plausibly thought to be a reliable measure of the dynamics of political mobilization and coalition formation of domestic organized interests favoring or resisting the removal of protectionist policies. Changes in the composition of domestic coalitions should thus affect policymakers' willingness to comply in a swift manner. Since I contend that a high degree

[1] Relevant data are missing for a subset of WTO defendants, including Thailand, Egypt, Guatemala, Argentina, Colombia, Chile, the Dominican Republic, Ukraine, and the Philippines. Collectively, these defendants account for over twenty cases, which are omitted from model due to lack of data on trade in intermediates.

of integration of the targeted sector into value chains crucially influences such domestic political dynamics of political mobilization by increasing the size of the domestic pro-trade liberalization coalition, it is plausible to expect time until incentives for policymakers to supply delay tactics should also decrease, ultimately increasing the likelihood of timely compliance.

I track the domestic policy result of the dispute and consider the ruling to be complied with if WTO-inconsistent measures are withdrawn or modified to be in line with WTO law. In the cases in which the Panel rulings were appealed, I consider the AB report as the final ruling that clarifies the extent of the violation and calculate the time from the circulation of the AB panel report to compliance by the defendant.[2] In cases where the defendant modified the relevant policy, instead of withdrawing it, and such modification was opposed by the complainant and taken to the compliance panels, I assess each compliance panel decision on its own. If the compliance panels found no evidence of violation (which means the defendant did indeed implemented the panel ruling(s) in good faith), I do not take into account the compliance panel stage when calculating the time until compliance. However, if the compliance panels ruled that there was non-compliance and the defendant was required to further change the modified measure(s), then I calculate the time from the appellate body report until the final modification that corrected the WTO-inconsistent measure(s). In the appendix, I provide examples of my approach and a corresponding chart that gives details of the different stages of the WTO panel process.[3]

[2] I start the clock to calculate "time until compliance" from the AB report because the extent of a violation, and therefore the extent of a policy change that is required to bring compliance is only clarified for the defendants after a final ruling is delivered by the AB. As a robustness check, however, I run separate analyses in my supplementary appendix in which I calculate the "time until compliance" from the original panels' report. The results are substantively similar.

[3] Four additional details warrant attention. First, in cases where there were multiple complainants in a dispute, I distinguish each pair and count them as separate disputes. This decision is consistent with a number of works in the field (e.g., Horn et al. 1999; Bagwell et al. 2004) and was made so that I can observe the impact of additional WTO members in a dispute. Second, my sample does not include disputes that targeted horizontal measures, since these disputes did not target specific sectors. Although some horizontal measures may involve certain sectors more than others, I only examine responses to litigation if there is a sector whose import dependence can be measured. Third, a few disputes resulted in compliance around the same time there was a panel ruling. Even though the defendants in these disputes did not comply with a panel ruling per se, they demonstrated

Some scholars have previously tried to measure DSM compliance by taking trade flows as a proxy (Bown 2004; Peritz 2016). There are several reasons why this measure is unreliable though since trade volumes are heavily affected by other factors, such as economic shocks, newly ratified Preferential Trade Agreements (PTAs), armed conflicts, sanctions between WTO Members, or the economic growth of disputants over the course of a long dispute, making an assessment of whether the WTO-illegal measures were modified a more reliable measure (Bown 2004, p. 814). Moreover, firms and sectors in complainants' economies may well adapt and substitute their markets when faced with market restricting barriers. Also, when taking an increase in trade volumes between a complainant and a defendant, one needs to assume that all disputes are about market access, which is not necessarily the case (Bown and Reynolds 2014, p. 44).

My main independent variable is the *targeted sector's level of integration into value chains*. I therefore take sectors as my unit of analysis in this section. This is due to two reasons. Firstly, from a theoretical standpoint, my independent variable should not be affected by the heterogeneity of firm preferences within sectors. I noted above—and through my previous works—that firms often politically mobilize through sector associations in response to WTO disputes (Yildirim 2017, 2018) because usually a number of firms—rather than one single firm—is affected by trade barriers targeted in WTO disputes. This means that sectors' level of integration into value chains captures many firms that are international and affected by a dispute. Secondly, I am not able to use firm-level data in response to WTO litigation due to data limitations. To the best of my knowledge, there is no cross-country panel data available on firms' political mobilization over WTO litigation—and it would be beyond a herculean task to create one. I therefore conduct sector-level analysis here and further elaborate on how firms enter into coalition in the following section through the case studies presented.

In order to measure sectors' level of GVC integration, I rely on the most comprehensive and reliable dataset that has sector-level global value

domestic policy change after a panel composition, in which the clarity of violations Ire most likely made before the circulation of panel reports. Finally, in certain disputes, defendants notified the WTO DSB of compliance, but I could not find the corresponding domestic legislation. These cases are coded "complied with" and I rely on WTO Members' notification to the DSB and official WTO records to consider the extent of compliance.

chain indicators, the OECD-WTO Joint Trade in Value Added Database (TiVA).[4] In order to do so, I first identify the sector(s) targeted in the disputes by examining original WTO documents submitted as part of the panel process. After identifying the targeted sectors in a dispute, I check my designation with the International Standard Industrial Classification (ISIC). Second, I use the ISIC code and match relevant sectors with TiVA data at the country-sector level. I focus on three alternative measures drawn from TiVA: the sectors' *total import dependence*, which measures affected sectors' imports as a share of GDP, *import dependence for intermediate goods*, which measures imports of intermediate products as a share of sector output, and finally *foreign value added share of gross exports*, which captures how much of a sector's exports actually consist of foreign value added.

These alternative measures tap into different components of value chain integration and focus on the role of imports in a sectors' final output and exports, capturing sectors' reliance on foreign products. Since my argument concentrates on the effects of value chain integration on the domestic politics of trade; *in casu*, on how different levels of integration affect the politics of compliance in WTO disputes, I use trade in both final *and* intermediate goods. Following the literature, I consider trade in intermediates especially to be the most important value chain-related factor influencing the domestic politics of trade, and the most straightforward measure of internationalization of production (Baccini et al. 2018; Eckhardt and Poletti 2016; Amador and Cabral 2014, p. 19). I show that my results are substantively similar across all three operationalizations.[5]

Drawing on the existing literature I highlighted above, I also include the following control variables.

Power asymmetry: I start by accounting for the possibility that patterns of compliance in WTO dispute settlement are affected by power asymmetries between the litigants and the differences in complainants' retaliatory capacity. In order to account for this confounding factor, I use three different measures. First, following Bown (2004), I examine the defendant's dependence on the complainant as an export market. I measure the

[4]The dataset is available at: https://www.oecd.org/sti/ind/measuring-trade-in-value-added.htm. Accessed on 20 June 2020.

[5]For the TiVA dataset, see http://stats.oecd.org/Index.aspx?DataSetCode=TIVA2015_C1#. Note that in cases where import data from TiVA was not available, UN COMTRADE database was used.

credibility of the retaliatory threat as the percentage of the defendant's total exports to the complainant's market. Data on *defendant export dependence* are drawn from the UN COMTRADE database. Second, I consider the *defendant's share of FDI stocks* in the complainant's market out of total FDI stocks. This should place additional pressure on the defendant to comply, in order to avoid potential retaliatory actions undertaken by the complainant in the form of discriminatory measures against defendant FDIs.[6] Lastly, I look at the power asymmetries between the defendant and the complainant by examining the differences in their GDP (Sattler and Bernauer 2011). To capture this, I collect GDP data from UNCTAD and subtract the log of defendant GDP from the log of complainant GDP for each dispute. It is important to note, however, that these two measures of power asymmetry, i.e., *share of FDI stocks* and *complainant's economic power* mirror the logic and captured by the threat of retaliation. I therefore do not include them in my main model but additional results including them can be found in the appendix, yielding similar results as in my main model.

Political mobilization: I also control for the possibility that the level of political mobilization engendered in the defendant by the WTO dispute might affect compliance. Ideally, and following Olson (1965), I would use measures that assess both whether a dispute touches upon an economically-important sector and whether the potential for political mobilization in such sector is high. The Herfindahl-Hirschman Index (HHI), which measures the level of concentration within a market, would nicely capture the logic that underlies this hypothesis.[7] Unfortunately, data to construct this measure across all considered disputes are not available. Other measures of the "political importance" of WTO disputes that have been proposed so far include the level of sector employment and whether the dispute targeted the agricultural sector.[8] I use the *targeted*

[6] The data on FDI stocks were collected from the OECD where available and from EUROSTAT for the EU. For data on developing WTO members, I utilized UNCTAD. The closest year available was used if data were missing for certain years.

[7] See OECD (1993), for an overview on HHI index and sector concentration.

[8] Sector employment is used as a proxy for political importance by Hoffman and Kim, "The Political Economy of Compliance in WTO Disputes," Unpublished Manuscript, 2009. Spilker (2012) and Sattler et al. (2014) consider agricultural sectors to be politically important.

sector's value added as a share of the defendant's GDP as a proxy for political mobilization because the literature on interest groups clearly suggests that sectoral value added largely predicts the intensity of lobbying (Messer et al. 2011; Berkhout et al. 2015).

Issue complexity: I account for the political importance of the dispute by looking into the nature of the disputed issues. Some analyses have shown that disputes over *complex* issues are less likely to be settled during the consultation stage of WTO litigation and are more likely to be impaneled (Guzman and Simmons 2002; Sattler et al. 2014). Scholars have also shown that certain measures challenged at the WTO—such as complex behind the border regulatory measures—are more difficult to comply (Brewster and Chilton 2014) since they cannot be partially negotiated for settlement and would require significantly longer administrative procedures for modification (Wilson 2007). High levels of issue complexity could therefore decrease the likelihood of a swift compliance by defendants following Panel or Appellate Body rulings. In line with the existing literature, I consider targeted measures as "non-complex" if they are quotas or subsidies, which can be corrected much more easily in comparison to complex issues such as administrative regulations and other behind the border measures (Guzman and Simmons 2002). My (non-)complexity measure takes a value of 0 if the issue is complex and 1 if it is simple.

Defendants' level of democracy: Although the arguments made under the so-called "democratic peace" have not been tested with regard to compliance in WTO disputes, I recognize the importance of domestic institutions in determining WTO Members' adherence to their international trade commitments (Mansfield et al. 2002). In order to account for this potential determinant of compliance, I control for the *level of democracy of the defendant* in each dispute relying on the widely-used Polity IV dataset (Marshall and Jaggers 2002).

Veto players: I also account for the number of domestic *veto players* in the defendant state, as they are considered a critical factor in influencing the general propensity of a political system to move away from the status quo (Tsebelis 2002). For non-EU countries, I rely on the Political Constraints (PolCon) database compiled by Henisz (2011). I use Henisz's method to compile a separate veto player score for the EU as a whole. This allows me to use a single variable that is consistent across

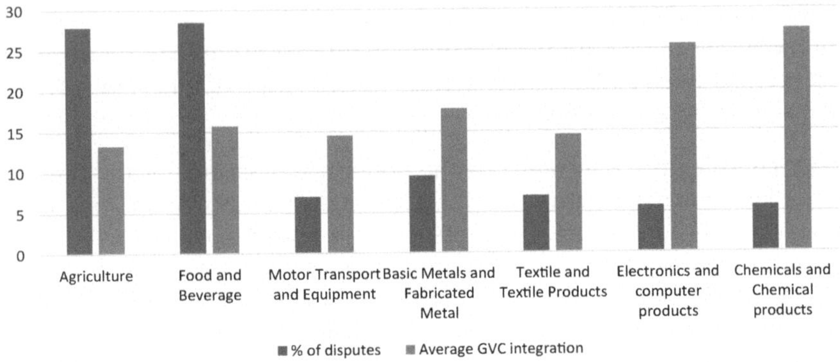

Fig. 3.1 Descriptive statistics by sector (*Source* Author's compilation from TiVA database)

disputes for all WTO Members. My calculation and the coding method for the EU can be found in the appendix.

Finally, I include separate dummy variables for whether the *US* or the *EU* are involved as defendants, to ascertain whether the results hold in cases in which these two particularly powerful trading entities are involved in a dispute.

I begin my investigation by examining the data on all WTO disputes between 1995 and 2016.[9] Fig. 3.1 summarizes two important variables, with respect to the seven main economic sectors. The blue bars, which depict the percentage of disputes that come from each sector, show that the most frequently targeted industries come from Agriculture, Production of Food and Beverages, and Manufacturing of Metals. This is not necessarily surprising as targeted sectors tend to be those that have traditionally been protected, such as farming or steel manufacturing.

The red bars, on the other hand, provide information on the average GVC integration of sectors by using the proxy of foreign value added in exports. In other words, we observe how much sectors have been using foreign imported products for their exports—averaged over time. I

[9] As mentioned in the introduction, the analysis here draws upon my previous work. It is particularly influenced by my doctoral dissertation and a co-authored article I published by the Review of International Organizations titled 'Internationalization of production and Compliance in WTO disputes'.

Table 3.1 Descriptive statistics for relevant variables

Variable	*Minimum*	*Maximum*	*Mean*	*Std. Dev.*
Compliance (months)	0	168	24.10	36.33
Foreign inputs in sector exports	3.36	54.86	18.73	9.28
Sectors' intermediate import dependence	0.01	3.34	0.35	0.46
Sectors' (total) import dependence	0.01	5.85	0.60	0.76
Defendant Polity score	−7	10	7.44	5.48
Defendant export dependence	0.01	88.59	13.78	20.82
Sector value added (logged)	0.01	9.83	1.59	1.49
Veto players	0.00	0.87	0.69	0.29

note that the level of integration is, in general, negatively correlated with the frequency of disputes, suggesting that disputes tend to arise around sectors that have lower levels of integration. This suggests that states are generally less likely to implement policies that conflict with WTO rules in sectors that are heavily integrated, except motor vehicles & transport equipment.

Table 3.1 provides additional descriptive statistics on the relevant features of disputes at the WTO (excluding dummy variables). My dependent variable ranges from immediate compliance to holdouts of more than 14 years. This indicates that while certain disputes result in very quick implementation, some drag along over a decade. My key independent variables, foreign inputs in sector exports, intermediate import dependence of sectors, and sector' reliance on imports show different levels of variation. While foreign value added in exports range from levels of 0.01% to nearly 55% (though 95% of observations remain under around 20% integration), import dependence show a relatively more modest variation between 0.01 and 5.85 and sectors' reliance on intermediate imports range between near-zero to 3.34.[10] Other variables show relatively broad ranges, with reasonable levels of variation.

Having briefly examined the data, I turn to my analysis. As my variable of interest is represented by the time until the defendant complies, I analyze the data using a semiparametric Cox proportional hazards model. The Cox model is advantageous in that it does not require specification of the baseline hazard function and that estimation of the partial likelihood

[10] Results remain substantively similar when omitting outliers.

Table 3.2 Results from Cox proportional hazard model

	Baseline	*Time included*	*Sector GVC included*	*Sector GVC included*	*Sector GVC included*
Def. democracy	0.10*	0.06	0.08	0.06	0.09
	(0.05)	(0.06)	(0.06)	(0.06)	(0.06)
Def. export Dependence	−0.01	−0.01	−0.01	−0.01	−0.01
	(0.01)	(0.01)	(0.01)	(0.01)	(0.01)
Issue complexity	0.85***	0.96***	1.06***	1.03***	0.93***
	(0.22)	(0.25)	(0.25)	(0.25)	(0.25)
Sectoral value added	−0.07	−0.10	−0.11	−0.14	−0.06
	(0.06)	(0.08)	(0.08)	(0.08)	(0.08)
Veto players	−3.02**	−2.04*	−2.68**	−2.57**	−2.23**
	(1.14)	(1.25)	(1.23)	(1.23)	(1.21)
EU defendant	−0.18	−0.36	−0.18	−0.09	−0.50
	(0.30)	(0.39)	(0.40)	(0.40)	(0.39)
US defendant	0.23	−0.04	0.10	0.16	−0.01
	(0.26)	(0.35)	(0.36)	(0.36)	(0.36)
Intermediate import dependence			0.67**		
			(0.23)		
Import dependence				0.48***	
				(0.14)	
Foreign inputs in exports					0.02*
					(0.01)
Num. obs.	136	136	136	136	136

*** $p < 0.01$, ** $p < 0.05$, * $p < 0.1$
Standard errors in parentheses; all tests are two-tailed tests

function with random right censoring of observations remains efficient (Efron 1977). It is also useful in that it can incorporate predictable time-varying covariates, provided that they enter into the model linearly.

Table 3.2 presents the results of my Cox regression across six different models.[11] Columns 1-3 represent different model specifications for the

[11] Replicatio files can be accessed through my website, www.aydinbyildirim.com.

WIOD dataset, while columns 4-6 use three different operationalizations of value chain integration from the TiVA data. Examination of the Schoenfeld residuals across all six models suggests that the proportional hazards assumption is satisfied in each case (Box-Steffensmeier et al. 2003). Interpretation of the results is straightforward: Positive values indicate that the variable is related to a higher probability of failure (i.e., compliance). Thus, factors with positive coefficients are associated with a shorter time until compliance. Column 1 depicts the baseline model, including all relevant covariates except for value chain integration. The results suggest that time until compliance is driven by issue complexity and EU membership, both of which are negatively related to time until compliance. The model in column 2 incorporates integration through my proxy variable, import dependence on intermediates. When I include this measure, I find that it also significantly reduces time until compliance. Additionally, I find significant effects several other factors: democracy, which makes compliance more likely, and veto players and sectoral value added, both of which increase the time to compliance. The effects of the previously-marginally-significant EU variable vanish. The effects of integration remain in my third model—where I include dummies for the year in which the dispute is initiated—as does sector value added. In addition, I see a marginal effect for US as a defendant. Accounting for time allows me to control for changes in the international system or in the nature of the disputed issues, as Ill as for institutional changes that might affect willingness to settle, such as the expiration of Article 13 of the WTO's Agriculture Agreement in 2004 (Goldstein 1996; Poletti et al. 2015). The inclusion of time dummies increases the magnitude of most coefficients, including value chain integration. I also find a consistently significant result for issue complexity, suggesting that simpler issues are resolved more quickly than are complex issues.

Columns 3-5 of Table 3.2 use the most complete specification from the model (column 2), and three different operationalizations of my key independent variable: intermediate import dependence, import dependence, and foreign value-added share in sector exports. My general results remain robust, with my value chain measures reaching statistical significance at the $p < 0.05$ level in each model. I find this robustness check to be especially encouraging. Taking into account different measures of GVC integration, I see that the outcome of compliance is positively affected in every model. Several additional observations note attention. First, the analysis shows that democracy becomes non-significant as I move on from the baseline model. This observation is interesting on its own and is consistent with my argument. Indeed, defendants in a WTO dispute seem to have better chances of complying swiftly if they are more consolidated democracies. Such tendency might very well be the case in certain disputes where economic costs are not too concentrated—perhaps disputes that are horizontal. In the absence of organized domestic interests, which are triggered by more concentrated economic costs in a dispute, we can expect democracies to be able to abide by their trade commitments relatively faster. Second, it is also important to note that the impact of threat of retaliation as a factor affecting time until compliance is the opposite from what the literature would suggest. I believe this is because a threat of retaliation is inherent in any dispute and all complainant WTO Members have credible retaliatory capacity—however small they may be. Even though there are differences in market sizes of complainants, they can all impose concentrated costs on defendant WTO Members and therefore all possess credible retaliatory capacity. Alternative measures of power and retaliatory capacity would be beneficial to single out the (potential) impact of this explanatory factor in the future. Third, I see that veto players and issue complexity remain significant factors—and have the hypothesized positive and negative signs—in every model, which testifies to their robustness.

The results in Table 3.2 can be interpreted relatively easily in terms of effects on the underlying hazard ratio. However, given the potential complexity of the hazard function and the semiparametric nature of the model, the substantive implications of my results can be difficult to grasp from examining a table. For this reason, it is instructive to examine the average predicted "risk" of compliance in disputes, given a change in levels of integration, which I aim to do below.

Figure 3.2 depicts the probability of compliance experienced by two different groups, i.e., sectors, given their level of dependence on foreign value added for their exports. I used the results from the model in column 5, and show how the "risk" of compliance is different for the two groups that have differences in their level of integration into value chains. The two lines indicate the two values of foreign value added in sectors' exports, long one showing the group with around 3% foreign value added and the shorter dotted line showing the group that is around 50% dependent on foreign value added for its exports. The upward trend in the risk of compliance for the highly integrated group is obvious and consistent with both the findings above and my hypothesized relationship.

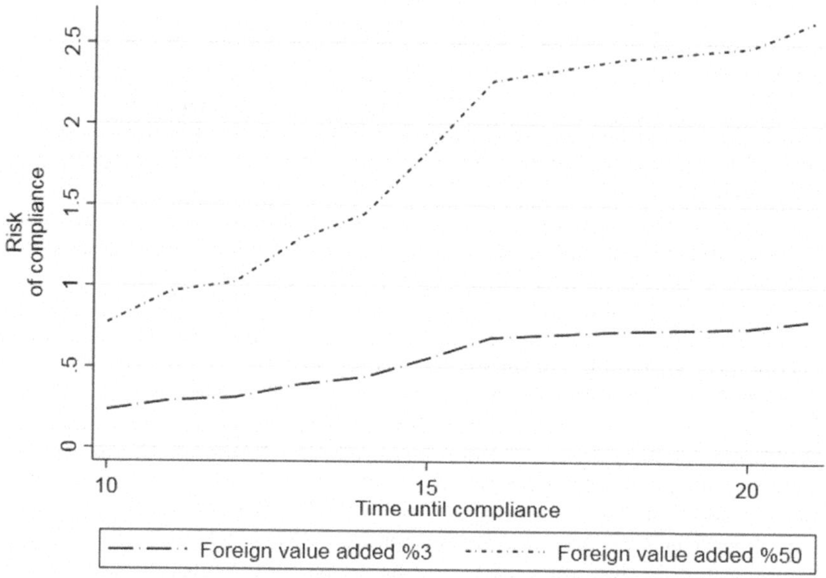

Fig. 3.2 Cumulative hazard function (*Source* Author's calculation)

On average, I observe that the probability of attaining DSB-mandated 15 months of compliance is significantly more likely when the affected sector is highly integrated into GVCs, in comparison with a sector that shows very low integration. It is important to note that the shape of the curve suggests that the impact of additional intermediate import dependence levels off after roughly two years into the dispute.

In sum, my analysis leads me to confirm the hypothesis I presented above. My results suggest that value chain integration plays a powerful role in a defendant's willingness to comply in WTO disputes. In addition to finding that the effect is statistically significant across over one hundred cases, I find large substantive effects, both on average, and when applied to specific instances. I also demonstrate that the marginal effect of import dependence is largest at low-to-moderate levels, suggesting that changes in integration have the greatest role to play at when states are becoming integrated into the world market. This is especially relevant, as some of the most widely-disputed sectors—agriculture, food and beverages, and textiles—tend to have relatively low levels of import dependence. One can postulate that increasing integration in these areas would likely lead to faster compliance with WTO rulings.

References

Amador, João, and S. Cabral. 2014. Global Value Chains Surveying Drivers and Measures. Working Paper 1739 (2014), European Central Bank (ECB), Frankfurt. Available at https://www.ecb.europa.eu/pub/pdf/scpwps/ecbwp1739.en.pdf?13f6d86f40a3c60325f27cbc08a18742. Accessed on March 22, 2016.

Baccini, L., A. Dür, and M. Elsig. 2018. Intra-Industry Trade, Global Value Chains, and the Political Economy of Preferential Trade Liberalization. *International Studies Quarterly* 62 (2): 329–340.

Bagwell, K., P. Mavroidis, and R. Staiger. 2004. The Case for Tradable Remedies in WTO Dispute Settlement. Discussion Paper No. 0405-05, Department of Economics, Columbia University, New York, NY.

Berkhout, J., B. Carroll, C. Braun, A.W. Chalmers, T. Destrooper, D. Lowery, S. Otjes, and A. Rasmussen. 2015. Interest Organizations Across Economic Sectors: Explaining Interest Group Density in the European Union. *Journal of European Public Policy* 22 (4): 462–480.

Bown, C. 2004. On the Economic Success of GATT/WTO Dispute Settlement. *The Review of Economics and Statistics* 86 (3): 811–823.

Bown, C., and K. Reynolds. 2014. Trade Flows and Trade Disputes. Policy Research Working Paper 6979, Development Research Team, World Bank, Washington.

Box-Steffensmeier, J., D. Reiter, and C. Zorn. 2003. Nonproportional Hazards and Event History Analysis in International Relations. *Journal of Conflict Resolution* 47 (1): 33–53.

Brewster, R., and A. Chilton. 2014. Supplying Compliance: Why and When the United States Complies with WTO Rulings. *Yale Journal of International Law* 39 (2): 201–247.

Busch, M., and E. Reinhardt. 2003. Transatlantic Trade Conflicts and GATT/WTO Dispute Settlement. In *Transatlantic Economic Disputes: The EU, The US, and the WTO*, ed. E. Petersmann and M. Pollack. Oxford: Oxford University Press.

Davey, A. 2005. Evaluating WTO Dispute Settlement: What Results Have Been Achieved Through Consultations and Implementation of Panel Reports? Research Paper 05-19, College of Law, University of Illinois, Chicago, IL.

De Bièvre, D., and A. Dür. 2005. Constituency Interests and Delegation in European and American Trade Policy. *Comparative Political Studies* 38 (10): 1271–1296.

Eckhardt, J., and A. Poletti. 2016. The Politics of Global Value Chains: Import Dependent Firms and EU-Asia Trade Agreements. *Journal of European Public Policy*. https://doi.org/10.1080/13501763.2015.1085073.

Efron, B. 1977. The Efficiency of Cox's Likelihood Function for Censored Data. *Journal of the American Statistical Association* 72 (359): 557–565.

Goldstein, J. 1996. International Law and Domestic Institutions: Reconciling North American "Unfair" Trade Laws. *International Organization* 50 (4): 541–564.

Grossman, G., and E. Helpman. 2001. *Special Interest Politics*. Cambridge: MIT Press.

Guzman, A., and B. Simmons. 2002. To Settle or Empanel? An Empirical Analysis of Litigation and Settlement at the WTO. *Journal of Legal Studies* 31 (1): 205–235.

Henisz, W.J. 2011. Political Constraints Database, data and code accessed via http://www-management.wharton.upenn.edu/henisz/.

Horn, H., H. Nordström, and P. Mavroidis. 1999. Is the Use of the WTO Dispute Settlement System Biased? Discussion Paper 2340, Centre for Economic Policy Research, London.

Hudec, R. 1993. *Enforcing International Trade Law: The Evolution of the Modern GATT Legal System*. Salem: Butterworth Legal.

Mansfield, E., H. Milner, and Peter Rosendorff. 2002. Why Democracies Cooperate More: Electoral Control and International Trade Agreements. *International Organization* 56 (3): 477–513.

Marshall, M., and K. Jaggers. 2002. Polity IV Project: Regime Characteristics and Transitions, 1800–2007. Available at http://www.systemicpeace.org/polity/polity4.htm. Accessed on April 12, 2016.

Messer, A., J. Berkhout, and D. Lowery. 2011. The Density of the EU Interest System: A Test of the ESA Model. *British Journal of Political Science* 41 (01): 161–190.

Olson, M. 1965. *The Logic of Collective Action. Public Goods and the Theory of Groups*. Cambridge, MA: Harvard University Press.

Organization for Economic Cooperation and Development (OECD). 1993. Glossary for Industrial Organisation Economics and Competition Law. Available at https://www.oecd.org/regreform/sectors/2376087.pdf. Accessed on February 15, 2016.

Peritz, L. 2016. When are International Institutions Effective? The Impact of Domestic Veto Players on Compliance with WTO Rulings. Paper Presented at the 9th Annual Meeting of the Political Economy of International Organizations. Salt Lake City, Utah.

Poletti, A., D. De Bièvre, and T. Chatagnier. 2015. Cooperation in the Shadow of WTO Law: Why Litigate When You Can Negotiate? *World Trade Review* 14 (S1): S33–S58.

Sattler, T., and T. Bernauer. 2011. Gravitation or Discrimination? Determinants of litigation at the World Trade Organization. *European Journal of Political Research* 50 (2): 143–167.

Sattler, Thomas, Gabriele Spilker, and Thomas Bernauer. 2014. Does WTO Dispute Settlement Enforce or Inform? *British Journal of Political Science* 44 (4): 877–902 (Published online in 2013).

Spilker, Gabriele. 2012. Compliance with WTO Dispute Rulings. Working Paper 2011-25, National Centre of Competence in Research Trade Regulation, Zurich, Switzerland.

Tsebelis, G. 2002. *Veto Players: How Political Institutions Work*. Princeton: Princeton University Press.

Wilson, B. 2007. Compliance by WTO Members with Adverse WTO Dispute Settlement Rulings: The Record to Date. *Journal of International Economic Law* 10 (2): 397–403.

Yildirim, Aydin. 2017. Domestic Political Implications of Global Value Chains: Explaining EU Responses to Litigation at the World Trade Organization. *Comparative European Politics*.

Yildirim, Aydin. 2018. Firms' Integration into Value Chains and Compliance with Adverse WTO Panel Rulings. *World Trade Review* 17 (1): 1–31.

CHAPTER 4

Firms, Coalitions, and WTO Disputes: Domestic Private Actors in the WTO

Abstract Under what conditions do defendant WTO Members swiftly implement adverse rulings of WTO panels? In this chapter, I bring forth an argument relying on qualitative evidence. I demonstrate that when a dispute touches upon the interests of firms and sectors integrated into value chains and targets import-restricting measures, these private actors are triggered to mobilize and press for compliance. The mobilization of these firms changes the domestic political conditions in favor of timely implementation. I show the plausibility of my argument in a comparative design with four case studies in which the US and Canada acted as defendants in WTO disputes. I control for a number of political factors and also consider legal sources of variation—i.e., the complexity of the form of implementation—that may impact WTO Members' record of compliance. This chapter thus complements the quantitative evidence presented and supports my theoretical proposition regarding firms' and sectors' value chain integration and mobilization over WTO dispute settlement rulings.

Keywords Case study · Canada · United States · Steel safeguards · Softwood lumber

Having established the impact of value chain integration from a large-n perspective, I focus on case studies in this chapter. Four cases involving the US and Canada as defendants are analyzed below to see if they fit the

A. B. Yildirim, *Value Chains and WTO Disputes*,
https://doi.org/10.1007/978-3-030-49094-2_4

hypothesis that affected firms' integration into value chains shorten the time until defendants comply with WTO rulings. I conduct case studies in order to trace the process in which firms lobby for their trade policy preferences in response to WTO litigation in defendant WTO Member economies. This method not only allows me to unpack the underlying mechanism of my argument but it also permits me to take advantage of firm-level data that is available for certain disputes. In addition, I am also able to consider legal sources of variation regarding different forms of legal actions WTO Members employ to implement panel rulings—which would have been extremely demanding to consider for a larger sample.

I employ Most Similar Systems Design (MSSD) to examine my cases (Przeworski and Teune 1970). This means for my case selection I keep all the potentially relevant factors constant except the variable(s) that I am interested—i.e., affected firms' level of integration into value chains. In line with the literature, I first take into account the defendant's level of democracy and examine disputes where the defendants were consolidated democracies. Second, I consider the impact of veto players and keep it constant in my comparisons—i.e., I initially compare two cases in which there were a low number of veto players whose consent was necessary to enact policy change, and then I compare two other cases with high veto players capacity. I use a similar control technique to take into account the complexity of the defendants' form of implementation as well. I initially compare two cases in which simpler forms of implementation were used by the defendants, and then I compare two cases in which defendants brought compliance via complex forms of implementation. By keeping these sources of variation constant, I am able to point out the potential impact of my primary explanatory variable and therefore explain how firms politically mobilize and shape the trade policy preferences of WTO Members.

Two additional (important) points warrant attention. First, I focus on the complexity of the form of implementation in this chapter and include it in the analysis with much more breadth and nuance. I pay special attention to the potential role of complexity because an in-depth case study allows me to look into this factor with a much more degree of precision. I can trace the procession of disputes and examine what legal forms of policies the defendants WTO Members used to comply with WTO rulings.

This provides a unique advantage to look at this source of variation in a detailed manner and I take this opportunity here.[1]

Second, I do not necessarily keep the power asymmetry between trade partners in this analysis as a constant. In other words, I did not specifically exclude relatively small economies because they are "powerless" against their larger counterparts. As I argued above, in WTO DSM litigants have credible retaliatory capacity even if they are not the largest of economies. Even though there are differences in market sizes of complainants, they can all impose concentrated costs on defendant WTO Members and therefore all possess credible retaliatory capacity.

My case selection thus involves highly democratic pairs which are also advanced economies—regardless of their size. I therefore narrow down the sample from which I can choose my cases to a subset of the population involving the US and Canada as defendants since they are consolidated democracies and involved in a large amount of disputes in which we can observe theoretically relevant variation. Moreover, among the disputes these three were involved in, I pick the cases that reflect the interaction of both the affected firms' degree of integration into value chains and the complexity of the form of implementation chosen by the defendants. Focusing on this variation along these two variables narrowed down my disputes to only a handful within which I had to make a decision. At that stage, I narrowed my selection to the disputes with the most available data, in order to avoid data limitations, and therefore chose the cases I present below.

In order to measure the political activity of firms highly integrated into value chains, I go beyond the operationalizations I outlined in the previous chapter involving large-n analysis. I focus on the import-dependence of the firms involved in the disputes as well as their foreign affiliation. In addition to scholarly publications, policy-oriented research, and secondary sources, such as media reports, I rely on two sets of data for my analysis. Firstly, I focus on official records from the WTO secretariat, non-governmental organizations (NGOs), and WTO Members such as dispute resolution memorandums, transcripts of legislative hearings, and

[1] I exhausted the ways in which I can take into account the number of veto players and the other variables found in the literature—the statistical analysis brought light into the potential impact of these relevant explanatory factors. Yet, the influence of "complexity" still remains underexplored in my opinion. This is also why I pay special attention to complexity here.

lobbying reports. Secondly, I turn to position papers, public statements, and lobbying spending statements made available by firms before, during, and after a WTO dispute. These data sources allow me to identify with much more detail the level of integration of firms into value chains and their political activity.

In order to measure the complexity of the form of implementation, I track the policies implemented by the defendants in my cases and consider how complex was the chosen form of implementation that brought the defendant in line with its WTO obligations. The nature and the operationalization of this variable deserve attention. From a legal perspective, compliance with adverse panel rulings may sometimes take longer because defendants employ a complex form of implementation. Since panels at the WTO DSM do not make policy proposal or legislative amendments, defendants are practically free to implement panels' recommendations in ways they seem fit (Mavroidis 2000). Article 3.7 of the Dispute Settlement Understanding (DSU) clearly states that the withdrawal of the measures found to be WTO-inconsistent is the first objective. Yet, this objective is simply a desirable outcome and does not invoke a legally binding suggestion; therefore, defendants often opt to modify the challenged measures instead of revoking it—bringing partial implementation (e.g., Pauwelyn 2000). Even though the panels *may* suggest the removal of the WTO-inconsistent measure or suggest other ways to implement the recommendations of the panels, this rarely occurs and ultimately the defendants can choose the legal form of implementation, as stated in Article 19.1 of the DSU.[2]

Therefore, I go beyond the nature of "complexity" I characterized in my previous analysis and focus on the form of implementation and

[2] With regard to a form of implementation, a WTO Members' "choice" implies a degree of freedom but this is barely the case. In order to modify or withdraw WTO-inconsistent measures, WTO Members have to employ legal actions that would correct the illegal measures. It would hardly be possible to correct a statute with an administrative measure, or a legislative act without a legislative amendment. I use the term "choice" here with this caveat. It is also important to note that a legally binding suggestion is exceptionally invoked in disputes involving subsidies because Article 4.7 of the Subsidies and Countervailing Measures (SCM) agreement clearly requests that WTO-illegal measure be "immediately withdrawn." Yet, even in this case the defendants may need different forms of implementation to withdraw the contested measure, depending on what the challenged measure is.

whether or not more complex forms of implementation create legal-administrative trouble for a defendant, causing it to take longer to carry out policy changes. In this dissertation, I consider forms of implementation to be "complex" based on three factors. First, I examine whether or not the implementing measure is an administrative or a legislative action. This is simply because administrative actions can be promulgated much faster than legislative ones (Wilson 2007). This conceptualization is consistent with my earlier notion of "complexity." I used this (relatively simplistic) characterization above in the large-n section and found it to be a significant factor. I take advantage of my in-depth design here and go beyond this binary distinction of "complexity" and consider others sources of variation that captures the complexity involving legislative changes. I consider the technical complexity of the measure in drafting it—e.g., if it requires developing new standards and examine the procedural steps involved in enacting the new measure, such as public hearings, committee meetings, and risk assessment procedures. Therefore, in cases where the form of implementation chosen by the defendant is a relatively complex one involving a complicated legislative change, then we would expect there to be a longer time before there has been compliance. In contrast, we can expect relatively simple measures—e.g., executive or administrative measures—that do not require longer legislative procedures to be implemented faster.

Yet, I aim to demonstrate that even legally complex forms of implementations can be fast tracked when the domestic conditions are more favorable to compliance. Although it is important to recognize the significance of complexity, my analysis demonstrates that defendant WTO Members do comply much faster when affected firms are integrated into value chains and push for swift implementation, regardless of the complexity of the form of implementation. This result shows that, domestic constituencies' preferences decisively shape WTO Members' responses to litigation at the DSM and governments sometimes comply quickly even in the face of complexity.

4.1 The Role of Firms in WTO Members' Responses to Litigation and the Impact of Affected Firms' Integration into Value Chains

The two comparative cases I studied reflect the necessary variation on my explanatory variables. In the first section, I examine the US responses to two disputes where number of veto players was low and the implementing measures were both executive actions—relatively simple forms of implementation—but the affected firms' value chain integration varied greatly. As briefly noted in the previous section, the steel sector is one with (relatively) high integration into value chains, especially considering foreign imported inputs used in various production processes, while the lumber (i.e., wood products) sector is relatively much lower in value chain integration. I demonstrate that even when employing simple forms of implementation; the US record of compliance was significantly different and can be explained by the affected firms' integration into global production networks. In the second section, I examine the responses of Canada to two disputes where the number of veto players was high and the implementing measures were complex regulatory changes. Yet I show that even in the face of complexity Canada brought swift compliance when affected firms were highly integrated into international production networks, which meant that these firms favored swift implementation and pressed their preferences to policymakers. This was especially the case for the pharmaceutical sector which shows one of the highest integration into value chains—see Fig. 3.1 in the previous chapter. The selected cases' variance on my two independent variables as well as their expected outcome is outlined in Table 4.1.

4.2 US Responses to Litigation

I start by comparing the response of the United States in the *US—Steel Safeguards* dispute lodged by the EU to its response in the *US—Softwood Lumber* disputes tabled by Canada.[3] The US complied with the panel rulings in both of these disputes with executive actions that required only a low number of veto players' consent, a presidential proclamation in the steel safeguards dispute and an executive agreement in the

[3] I examine all the lumber disputes lodged by Canada together—since they were all from the same complainant and were resolved together via one agreement.

Table 4.1 Characteristics of the selected cases and expected results

	Relatively simple form of implementation (low number of veto players)	*Complex form of implementation (high number of veto players)*
Affected firms show higher value chain integration	*US—Steel safeguards* Result: Swift implementation	*Canada—Pharmaceuticals* Result: Swift implementation
Affected firms show lower value chain integration	*US—Lumber* Result: Delayed implementation	*Canada—Dairy products* Result: Delayed implementation

softwood lumber disputes. Yet, the time it took for the US to implement the WTO panels' rulings in these two cases varied greatly; while in the softwood lumber disputes it took the US some 3 years to comply with the panels' recommendations, the steel dispute ended in compliance after only a few months—see Tables 4.2 and 4.3 for these two disputes'

Table 4.2 Overview of US—Steel safeguards

March 2002	The EU and other litigants request consultations with the US at the WTO with regard to the safeguards measures on imported steel
June 2002	WTO dispute challenging the barriers is impaneled (joined by many other WTO Members)
March 2003	Firms depending on steel imports rally behind the Consuming Industries Trade Action Coalition (CITAC), who lobbies the US Senate House Ways and Means Committee for an ITC investigation into the impact of safeguards
July 2003	WTO Panel ruling finds the safeguards measures WTO-inconsistent
November 2003	WTO Report of the Appellate Body largely upholds the findings and asks the US for compliance
	US Steel, Nucor Corp lobbies for non-compliance. The US Steelworkers' Union supports non-compliance
	CITAC counter-mobilizes. ITC investigation reveals steel safeguards cause significant injury to import-dependent firms
	WTO authorizes retaliation
December 2003	The US complies with the WTO ruling and the enacted barriers are removed through a presidential proclamation

Table 4.3 Overview of US-Lumber

August 2001–December 2002	Canada challenges US softwood lumber import regime at the WTO with successive disputes at the WTO (DS 236, 247, 257, 264, 277)
August 2002	The US import restricting measures found WTO inconsistent by the panels
September 2002	The import-competing firms rally behind the US Lumber Coalition and demand the US to appeal the WTO rulings
October 2003	Ad hoc organization representing wood-consumers, the Alliance for American Consumers for Affordable Homes (ACAH) asks for compliance
2004	AB panels largely uphold original panel rulings
December 2004–May 2005	The US claims compliance by lowering import duties, Canada disagrees and asks for a compliance panel
2005–February 2006	The USLC spends its largest ever lobbying spending. Labor organizations the Western Council of Industrial Workers comes out in support of USLC, as well as several senators
2005–2006	Compliance panels eventually side with Canada and the WTO paves the way to authorize 200 Million CAD in retaliatory tariffs
July 2006	The US demands Canada to give up 1 billion USD of the collected duties (half of them to be distributed to USLC members)
September 2006	The US brings compliance and the Softwood Lumber Agreement of 2006 is reached

timelines in comparison.[4] An examination of these two cases reveals that the domestic political environment with respect to *US—Steel Safeguards* favored swift implementation, due to the fact that the affected firms, which were highly integrated into value chains, mobilized and lobbied policymakers for compliance in addition to exporters who faced retaliatory sanctions. The dispute triggered the mobilization of import-dependent firms that were using imported steel products for their productions and the knock on effect of the barrier raised on the request of the US steel sector prompted them to mobilize and demand compliance in order to access cheaper imports. In contrast, the *US—Softwood Lumber* disputes

[4] The average time, in months, for the US to comply with adverse panel rulings is 21 months—by my own calculations. This means that the US's compliance in *US—Steel Safeguards* was significantly faster than usual, while its compliance in response to *US—Softwood Lumber* disputes was significantly slower.

resulted in compliance being extremely delayed because the domestic interests greatly favored protectionism. The lumber sector in the US was characterized by very low import dependence, consisting of firms that showed little or no integration into value chains. These import-competing firms favored protectionism in order to shield their domestic production from foreign competition. Without any substantial opposing pressure, the government of the US catered to the demands of the lumber sector by resisting compliance.

4.2.1 *The US' Swift Compliance with Panel Rulings*

In response to the demands of the domestic steel sector that rallied behind American Iron and Steel Institute, the United States Trade Representative (USTR) Robert Zoellick petitioned a Section 201 investigation to be carried out by the International Trade Commission (ITC) in June 2001 in order to determine the alleged injury caused by imports to US steel firms (USITC 2001; Read 2005). The objective of the investigation was to establish whether or not the US should impose emergency safeguard measures to a broad range of steel imports and protect the US steel sector from further harm. The investigation found "substantial injury" being caused by a number of imported steel products and the ITC made several recommendations as a remedy (USITC 2001). Considering the economic downturn of 2000, the poor competitive condition of the US steel sector, and to appease his constituencies in the face of the upcoming mid-term elections, President George W. Bush announced on March 5, 2002, that the US would impose several safeguard measures on steel imports, up to 30 percent tariffs and some additional tariff quotas—measures that were significantly harsher than the recommendations of the ITC (Bush 2002).

Unsurprisingly, the safeguard measures generated harsh responses from the US's major trade partners, especially from the EU, which tabled a WTO dispute in June 2002, later joined by Brazil, China, Japan, Korea, New Zealand, Norway, and Switzerland, which initiated separate disputes and argued that the imposed safeguard measures on steel violated a number of GATT articles as well as the WTO Agreement on Safeguards.[5] The WTO panels found that even though US steel sector was

[5] More specifically, Articles 2.1, 2.2, 3.1, 3.2, 4.1, 4.2, 5.1, 5.2, 7.1 and 9.1 of the Agreement on Safeguards and Articles I:1, XIII and XIX:1 of GATT 1994. See WTO disputes, DS248, DS249, DS251, DS252, DS253, DS254, DS258, DS259.

negatively affected by imports to a certain extent, the enacted safeguard measures were inconsistent with both GATT 1994 and WTO Agreement on Safeguards—a decision appealed by the US and mostly upheld by the Appellate Body (AB).[6]

The WTO dispute spurred political mobilization of import-dependent firms integrated into value chain networks, which had been fiercely opposing the safeguard measures since the complaint was lodged at the ITC. Firms that were consuming steel products, especially the manufacturers of motor vehicles and vehicle parts, argued that they were harshly affected by the safeguard measures, given their impact on production costs. Rallying behind the Consuming Industries Trade Action Coalition (CITAC), which created a "steel task force" to lift the ban on steel imports, steel consumers "strongly urged the Bush Administration to review immediately the economic impacts and unintended consequences of its decision to impose steel tariffs and act to end this tax on steel-using industries as quickly as possible" (CITAC 2002). Indeed, safeguard measures not only caused the price of certain steel products to increase by some 20%, but certain steel products were not readily available due to the tariff quotas and the domestic producers could not replace these specialized components (Francois and Baughman 2001). As the WTO dispute proceeded, the members of the CITAC "steel task force" continued their lobbying efforts and gathered the support of over 60 members of the US House of Representatives and convinced the Ways and Means Committee to request an ITC investigation on the impact of the safeguards on steel consumers,[7] which later highlighted the adverse effects of the measures on steel prices, as well as employment in the steel-consuming sectors (USITC 2003). Testifying to the Joint Economic Committee of the Congress, US Federal Reserve Chairman Alan Greenspan also sided with CITAC members, asking for the removal of the tariffs on steel products (Greenspan 2003).

[6] Appellate Body Report, *United States—Definitive Safeguard Measures on Imports of Certain Steel Products*, WT/DS248/AB/R, adopted 10 December 2003. The AB report was applicable to the other disputes as well.

[7] PR Newswire, *House Ways & Means Committee Formally Requests International Trade Commission to Analyze Impact of Steel Tariffs on Steel Consumers*. Accessed March 19, 2003, via: http://www.prnewswire.com/news-releases/house-ways--means-committee-formally-requests-international-trade-commission-to-analyze-impact-of-steel-tariffs-on-steel-consumers-74724457.html.

As the WTO dispute progressed, firms integrated into value chains continued putting pressure on the US government to lift the WTO-inconsistent measures. During a heated debate in US House of Representatives' Subcommittee on Trade, Mitsubishi, along with the global car-parts manufacturer Delphi and Metaldyne, pleaded the US government for the safeguard measures to be removed. These import-dependent firms heavily criticized the domestic steel producers for the injury they caused to their operations. In the words of the CEO of Metaldyne;

> They do not understand, or worse choose to ignore, how the manufacturing supply chain works, particularly in the automotive sector. The truth of the matter is that domestic steel producers are neither approved sources, nor in some cases do they have the capacity or capability to supply some of our requirements despite what they told the Department of Commerce that they could. (Leuiliette 2003)

The coalition of firms requesting the removal of the safeguard measures further included other steel consumers, such as Sharp, Energizer, and many small and mid-sized enterprises.[8] Therefore, the pressure on the government to withdraw the safeguard measures was mounting rather quickly.

In response, the domestic steel producers counter-mobilized but met with no success. The American Iron and Steel Institute, which was behind the original ITC investigation, as well as major American producers such as the Nucor Corporation and US Steel Corporation, worked together with the United Steel Workers Association (USWA) to put pressure on the government to keep the safeguard measures in place (Read 2005). The president of USWA, who was arguing that it was not time "to be inflicting further damage on the steel industry," came out, unsurprisingly, in opposition to compliance with the WTO panel ruling and stated that steelworkers' retirement schemes and health benefits depended on the tariffs being kept.[9] In contrast, CITAC starkly opposed any continuing imposition of duties and the President of the association pleaded "for the

[8] See The proceedings of the *Impact of the Section 201 Safeguard Action on Certain Steel Products*. Hearing before the U.S. House of Representatives Committee on Ways and Means Subcommittee on Trade, March 26, 2003.

[9] Elizabeth Becker, "W.T.O. Rules U.S. Tariffs on Steel Are Illegal," *The New York Times*. Accessed on November 10, 2003, via: http://www.nytimes.com/2003/11/10/business/worldbusiness/wto-rules-us-tariffs-on-steel-are-illegal.html.

sake of the US manufacturing sector, it's time to end the tariffs now" after increasing its lobbying spending with almost half a million USD from 2001 to 2003.[10] In addition, vehicle-parts manufacturers, including Metaldyne, Dura Automotive Systems, Textron, similarly demanded the lifting of the barriers.[11]

At the same time, the WTO ruling mobilized US exporters. Indeed, the cleverly-designed EU retaliatory measures targeted important US exports such as Florida citrus, Louisiana rice, California nuts, and North Carolina pajamas, which were politically-organized sectors, located in states important to the upcoming presidential election in 2004 (Jacobs 2016). Moreover, other heavy-industry exporters, including Harley Davidson, were also lobbying for the resolution of the dispute to avoid retaliatory sanctions (Bown 2009, p. 101). As a result, the trade-liberalizing preferences of firms that are integrated into value chains were now seconded by exporters who wanted to avoid EU countermeasures, and thus shared the same policy objectives in achieving the removal of safeguard measures.

Facing the possibility of authorized retaliation from the EU and the domestic conditions heavily tilted in favor of compliance, the US swiftly implemented the panel ruling and the USTR Robert Zoellick announced on December 4, 2003 that US safeguard measures were to be lifted because "the domestic costs of the measures now outweighed their benefits" (Zoellick 2003). Even though it was general knowledge that President Bush prolonged the dispute in order to garner support for the upcoming 2004 elections, the decision to comply with the WTO ruling was exceptionally expedited thanks to the mobilization of firms integrated into production networks. These firms' efforts incentivized the US government to remove trade restricting barriers in a timely fashion, rather than to resist compliance until at least the election was over in late 2004.

[10] "U.S. Disagrees with the WTO Steel Ruling," *The World Trade Review*, 15 December 2003. Accessed on January 9, 2017, via: http://www.worldtradereview.com/news.asp?pType=N&iType=A&iID=72&siD=23&nID=12206.

[11] Tonya Vinas "DDayFor Steel," *Industry Week*, December 21, 2004. Accessed on May 12, 2016 via: http://www.industryweek.com/none/d-day-steel. See also Annual Lobbying by CITAC, Center for Responsive Politics. Accessed on December 12, 2016, via: https://www.opensecrets.org/lobby/clientsum.php?id=F12987&year=2001.

In conclusion, I confirm my hypothesis that highly international firms enter into a coalition with exporters and seek the removal of trade-restricting barriers targeted in WTO litigation. The domestic conditions were conducive for compliance because firms heavily integrated into value chain networks were able to mobilize and demand the removal of the trade barriers in addition to exporters who feared retaliatory sanctions. The position of these firms stemmed from their wish to access imports without quotas and tariffs. Since the safeguard measures increased their cost of production, these import-dependent firms quickly mobilized and pressed their preferences on US policymakers. The policymakers, in turn, were able to overcome the pressure from the import-competing firms and the domestic balance of interests was tilted in favor of immediate compliance.

4.2.2 *The US's Delayed Compliance Despite a "Simple" Form of Implementation*

In contrast to its behavior in the *US—Steel Safeguards* dispute, the US responded to the adverse panel rulings in *US—Softwood lumber* disputes with protracted non-compliance. Despite utilizing an executive measure to correct its WTO-inconsistent import regime on softwood lumber from Canada, the US government resisted complying with the WTO rulings for some three years until finally it changed the relevant domestic policies through the Softwood Lumber Agreement (SLA) in 2006. A close examination of the US's response to these successive disputes launched by Canada reveals that the domestic balance of interests in the US heavily favored non-compliance. The softwood lumber sector in the US was characterized by very low import-dependence and consisted of import-competing firms who were mobilized via the US Lumber Coalition (USLC) and pressed for protectionist measures. There were only a few retailer firms that counter-mobilized in an ad hoc manner against USLC and demanded a lifting of the import barriers. Therefore, the domestic balance of interests favored the import-competing producers and the US resisted complying with the adverse panel rulings for some three years, even though the WTO-inconsistent measures were modified with an executive agreement without the involvement of the Congress, which should have been capable of implementing the panels' recommendations much faster.[12]

It would be futile to attempt to examine the entirety of the "lumber saga" between the US and Canada in this article. This "grandfather of all trade disputes between the US and Canada" consisted of six different WTO lawsuits, several NAFTA disputes, and dates back to the 1960s.[13] I will only focus on the formal WTO disputes that were initiated by Canada between 2000 and 2002, which were all resolved via the SLA signed by both parties in 2006. The six WTO disputes lodged by Canada against the US mainly targeted the US Department of Commerce's (USDOC) treatment of export restraints as subsidies and its calculations of anti-dumping (AD) and countervailing duties (CVDs).[14] The WTO disputes were all initiated by Canada at the request of the Canadian softwood lumber producers when the US–Canadian Softwood Lumber Agreement of 1995 expired in 2001. This executive agreement was to be renewed by the US President but after garnering intense lobbying from USLC who received the support of some 51 senators directly asking the President not to renew it (Zhang and Laband 2003, p. 408), the agreement was discontinued.

The termination of the agreement meant that the Canadian exporters of softwood lumber faced combined duties of 27%, which prompted the Canadian government to bring the issue to international adjudication with the help of its domestic lumber sector (Charron 2005). In response to the challenge brought by Canada with regard to the treatment of export restraints as subsidies, the WTO panels in Lumber I and Lumber II

[12] The Softwood Lumber Agreement was an executive agreement was lobbied by some 51 senators directly asking him to not renew the Softwood Lumber Agreement of 1996 (Zhang and Laband 2003, p. 408).

[13] For a detailed overview, see Zhang (2007).

[14] Request for consultations, *United States—Measures Treating Export Restraints as Subsidies*, WT/DS194/1. Request for consultations, *United States—Preliminary Determinations with Respect to Certain Softwood Lumber from Canada*, WT/DS236/1. Request for consultations, *United States—Provisional Anti-Dumping Measure on Imports of Certain Softwood Lumber from Canada*, WT/DS247/1. Request for consultations, *United States—Final Countervailing Duty Determination with respect to certain Softwood Lumber from Canada*, WT/DS257/1. Request for consultations, *United States—Final Dumping Determination on Softwood Lumber from Canada*, WT/DS264/1. Request for consultations, *United States—Investigation of the International Trade Commission in Softwood Lumber from Canada*, WT/DS277/1.

exonerated the US.[15] However, consecutive panels mainly found that the USDOC's determination of injury and calculation of ADs and CVDs were inconsistent with the US's obligations under the SCM Agreement and the WTO Anti-Dumping Agreement—although the panels reiterated that Canadian lumber was indeed subsidized.[16] The decisions of the panels were largely upheld by the AB in all the disputes, which meant that, as of August 2004, the US had to change its import regime with regard to softwood lumber from Canada or face authorized retaliation.

However, the US resisted compliance for almost three years. The USLC, composed of large timber and lumber producers across the US, such as Sierra Pacific Industries, Potlatch Corp., and Plum Creek Timber Corp.,[17] engaged in intense lobbying both throughout the disputes and after the panel rulings to make sure the US did not cave into to the demands of the Canadian lumber exporters. As the dispute was progressing, USLC pressed and convinced the US government to appeal the WTO decision in 2002, which found the US calculation of subsidies WTO-inconsistent, with the chairman of the coalition calling the panel's decision "ridiculous" (USLC 2002a). As the appeals phase of the dispute went on, the US and Canada negotiated for a settlement, but met with no success. The USLC, which was continuing its campaign to protect US producers, stated that Canadians "have further undermined fair and free trade" (USLC 2002b) and lobbied the US government for further changes in the levels of tariffs on lumber as well as a reduction in the proposed cap on Canadian market share in the US lumber sector (USLC 2003). The demands of USLC were angrily rejected by the Canadians,

[15] See *US—Softwood Lumber I (WT/DS194) and US—Softwood Lumber II (WT/DS221).*

[16] More specifically, the WTO panel in *US—Softwood Lumber III* found that the US imposition of provisional AD duties were inconsistent with Articles 1.1 (b), 10, 14, 14 (d), 20.6, 17.3, and 17.4, and 17.1(b) SCM Agreement. The panel in *US—Softwood Lumber IV* found that the USDOC Final Countervailing Duty Determination was inconsistent with Articles 10, 14, 14(d) and 32.1 SCM Agreement and Article VI:3 of GATT 1994. The Panel in *US—Softwood Lumber V* found that the USDOC failed to comply with the requirements of Articles 2.4.2 of the Anti-Dumping Agreement by applying "zeroing" methodology. Finally, in *US—Softwood Lumber VI,* the panel ruled that the US violated Articles 3.5 and 3.7 the Anti-Dumping Agreement and Article 15.5 and 15.7 of the SCM Agreement.

[17] For an extensive list, see Barrie McKenna, "Members of U.S. Lumber Lobby Exposed," *The Globe and Mail*, January 12, 2006.

Pierre Pettigrew, then-trade-minister of Canada, stating that their differences were too large and the USLC "have excessive demands, once again" that Canada was not willing to meet.[18]

Around the time the negotiations were halted, the WTO AB circulated its ruling on two different disputes that largely upheld the findings of the original panels.[19] In response, the US attempted to satisfy its trade partner by revising the USDOC calculations and lowering the CVD duties to around 13%, bringing the combined duties down to roughly 20% (Briggs et al. 2005), which it said brought its softwood import regime into compliance. Canada heavily disagreed and subsequently asked a compliance panel to rule on the USDOC's revision. Meanwhile, there was some counter-mobilization from the US consumers of lumber and tinder, which rallied behind the Alliance of American Consumers for Affordable Homes and the National Home Builders Association, which asked the USDOC to comply with the WTO rulings and lower the AD duties applied to lumber from Canada (ACAH 2003). Although the prompt formation of this coalition to pressure the government was a clear indication of import-dependent firms' ability to mobilize, they were unable to convince the US government to change its domestic policies, as they were very small in number and had limited capital. In contrast, USLC stepped up its lobbying activities and from 360,000 USD reported lobbying spending in 2001, massively increased its lobbying spending to 737,000 USD in 2004 and a staggering 1.4 million USD in 2005—the largest amount it had ever spent in a single year.[20] It became clear that the efforts of USLC were bearing fruit as in the US Senate Committee on Commerce, Science, and

[18] "Canada, U.S. Softwood Talks Break Down," *Canada Broadcasting Corporation*, February 26, 2003. Accessed on December 2, 2017 via: http://www.cbc.ca/news/canada/canadaussoftwoodtalksbreakdown1.368117. See also "Lumber Talks Break Down," *The Globe and Mail*, February 26, 2003. Accessed on December 2, 2016 via: http://www.theglobeandmail.com/report-on-business/lumber-talks-break-down/article4127106/.

[19] Appellate Body Report, *United States—Final Countervailing Duty Determination with respect to certain Softwood Lumber from Canada*, WT/DS257/AB/R, adopted 17 February 2004. Appellate Body Report, *United States—Final Dumping Determination on Softwood Lumber from Canada*, WT/DS264/AB/R, adopted 31 August 2004. Around the same time the panel report on Lumber VI was also adopted, see Panel Report, *United States—Investigation of the International Trade Commission in Softwood Lumber from Canada*, WT/DS277/R, adopted 26 April, 2004.

[20] Center for Responsive Politics OpenSecrets database. The U.S. Fair Lumber Coalition lobbying spending. Accessed on March 22, 2016, via: https://www.opensecrets.org/lobby/firmsum.php?id=D000049396&year=2005.

Transportation hearing, the chairing senators Burns, Smith, and Snowe, who were representing the lumber-producing states of Montana, Oregon, and Maine, were all supporting USLC.[21] Moreover, the labor organization representing sawmills and lumber producers, the Western Council of Industrial Workers, also sided with the coalition.[22]

At the same time exporters who were worried about retaliation politically mobilized, but their political action did not bring about enough pressure to induce compliance.[23] Canadians revealed that a number of products in different sectors were being considered for cross-retaliation, including Californian wine, orange juice from Florida, and corn products from the Southern states—in addition to apparel and food products that were targeted under the Byrd Amendment dispute around the same time.[24] In response, wineries in the US (who also had Canadian affiliates that they were exporting to) demanded compliance to avoid any duties to their exports.[25] In addition, American Apparel and Footwear Association, who represents the apparel and footwear industries, also demanded that the US brought an end to the dispute by explicitly stating that they fear retaliation, in addition to food exporters who started to suffer from trade

[21] See the proceedings of the *Economic Impacts of the Canadian Softwood Lumber Dispute on U.S. Industries* hearing before the United States Senate Subcommittee on Trade, Tourism, and Economic Development, February 14, 2006.

[22] Ibid.

[23] Note that Canada was also considering retaliatory actions against the US as a result of the disputes regarding the so-called Byrd Amendment that was found to be WTO-illegal. It seems the potential sanctions lists were prepared together to take advantage of the Canada's victory in both disputes—see Inside US Trade, "U.S. Lumber Producers Prepare Defense of Byrd Law in Canada Suit," March 4, 2005. Accessed on March 21, 2017, via: https://insidetrade.com/inside-us-trade/us-lumber-producers-prepare-defense-byrd-law-canada-suit.

[24] American Journal of Transportation, August 28, 2005, "Canada Eyeing US Corn in Softwood Lumber Battle." Accessed on May 21, 2017, via: https://www.ajot.com/news/canada-eyeing-us-corn-in-softwood-lumber-battle. See also, "Canada Weighs Penalizing Long List of U.S. Goods," *New York Times*, November 24, 2004. Accessed on January 22, 2017, via: http://query.nytimes.com/gst/fullpage.html?res=9901E7D8173EF937A15752C1A9629C8B63. See Rus (2007) for details on the WTO dispute involving the Byrd Amendment and the sanctions the US faced.

[25] Simon Tuck and Campbell Clark, "Wine Industry Fears It Will Get the Lumber," August 25, 2005. Accessed on May 21, 2017, via: https://www.theglobeandmail.com/report-on-business/wine-industry-fears-it-will-get-the-lumber/article985300/.

sanctions.[26] Yet, the exporters' mobilization fell short of countering the influence of the lumber producers.

Still resisting the liberalization of its softwood lumber trade, the pressure upon the US government to comply with its international commitments was mounting quickly by the end of 2005. The Article 21.5 panels established at the request of Canada mostly found that the US was in non-compliance on 1 August 2005 and Canada requested the authorization to impose 200 million CAD in retaliatory tariffs.[27] In addition, with NAFTA panels also finding the US at fault and USLC losing its domestic litigation battle against the Canadian exporters (Reif 2007), the US was facing ever more pressure to change its domestic policies and bring them into line with its international commitments.

The US eventually brought compliance on September 12, 2006 after a fresh round of negotiations that disproportionately benefited USLC.[28] It was revealed in early 2006 that the US had around 5.4 billion USD in duties collected from Canadian exporters since 2001. The Canadians were arguing that in addition to a change in US domestic policy, the collected duties should be transferred back to Canada; but the US was demanding that some of the collected duties be distributed to US producers as compensation. Although Canada was unhappy with the arrangement, both sides reached a framework agreement in July 2006 and it was revealed that 1 billion USD would remain in the US, of which half would be distributed to US producers (Fergusson 2011). Three months later, the US Court of International Trade ironically ruled that the US actually had no right to keep any part of the collected duties, which the Canadians said they "gave away."[29] It is, of course, no surprise that the Americans argued that the legal decision was to be considered moot since the agreement was already signed, and half of the 1 billion were to be distributed

[26] See, among others, statements by American Apparel and Footwear Association and General Mills, delivered for the Technical Corrections to U.S. Trade Laws and Miscellaneous Duty Suspension Bills, U.S. Subcommittee on Trade of the Committee on Ways and Means U.S. House of Representatives, 109th Congress, September 2, 2005.

[27] WT/DS257/16.

[28] "Bush Ties Border Controls to Prosperity," *The Associated Press*, March 31, 2006. Accessed on September 13, 2017, via: http://www.nbcnews.com/id/12094377/ns/world_newsamericas/t/bushtiesbordercontrolsprosperity/#.V1VaKZF97IU.

[29] "Court Orders U.S. to Repay All $5.3 Billion in Softwood Duties," *The Vancouver Sun*, October 15, 2006. Accessed on July 22, 2016, via: http://www.canada.com/vancouversun/news/business/story.html?id=7a3d8697fa6a4efdb1de3ecb2fc5485d.

to USLC members.[30] With the US lumber lobby being satisfied with four years of protection and a cash inflow of 500 million USD, the US finally changed its import regime on softwood lumber from Canada with the Softwood Lumber Agreement of 2006, which brought the US into line with its WTO commitments and put an end to the disputes on the 12th of September.

In conclusion, the examination of this case further helps corroborate my hypothesis. I showed that the US compliance with adverse panel rulings in the *US—Softwood lumber* disputes was protracted because the firms affected by the dispute mobilized in favor of protectionist measures. Operating in a highly concentrated lumber market with major producers competing with imports, the US lumber producers were able to press the policymakers to back their protective demands, and even though there was some counter-mobilization from import-dependent firms, their small ad hoc organization was not able to challenge the influence of the lumber lobby. The targeted measures involved mostly the firms with little or no integration into value chains, and therefore the domestic conditions were very unfavorable to compliance. Even though the negotiated resolution to the dispute was a domestic policy change in the form of an executive agreement, the US strongly resisted implementing the panel rulings. Although the US's early resistance to compliance could potentially be attributed to the Bush administrations' efforts to garner support from the US lumber producers for the upcoming 2004 election, post-election behavior of the US remained unchanged. The administration resisted compliance even in the face of retaliation two years after the election period, therefore, it would be safe to assume that electoral concerns were not decisive in shaping the US's behavior regarding compliance in the *US—Softwood lumber* disputes against Canada.

4.3 Canada's Response to WTO Litigation

Having examined the US' responses to two disputes involving simpler forms of implementation, where the US' record of compliance significantly differed due to the affected firms' integration into value chains, I now turn to examine two disputes launched against Canada, both of

[30] "Final Lumber Deal Circumvents Opposition of Canadian Producers," *Washington Tariff and Trade Letters* 26 (41), October 16, 2006. Accessed on August 11, 2016, via: http://www.wttlonline.com/ht/a/GetDocumentAction/id/21605.

Table 4.4 Overview of Canada—Dairy products

October–December 1997	New Zealand and the US request consultations with Canada with regards to the Canadian special milk class scheme
May 1999	WTO panel rules Canadian measures WTO inconsistent
October 1999	AB upholds the ruling and Canada is asked to bring compliance
August–December 2000	Sector organizations and large international firms lobby in favor of non-compliance—, Ontario Dairy Farmers, McCain Foods
	Milk Producers of Quebec seeks local litigation to halt policy change
February 2001	Canada attempts to comply by introducing "commercial milk licenses." New Zealand and the US disagree, ask for a compliance panel
July 2002	Compliance panels find Canada's new measures still inconsistent with WTO law
January 2003	AB upholds the compliance panel ruling that was appealed by Canada
March 2003	Ontario farmers and SMEs lobby the government to resist compliance as well as PLQ
	More time is given to Canadian provinces to bring their legislation in line with WTO law
May 2003	Canada finally abolishes the commercial export milk scheme and complies with its WTO obligations

which instead involved complex forms of implementation and required the consent of high number of veto players in Canada. I examine the dairy products dispute tabled by the US and New Zealand and the dispute involving patent protection of pharmaceutical products lodged by the EU. Both of these disputes resulted in an adverse panel ruling and Canada implemented the panels' recommendations in response to both decisions with complex regulatory changes. However, the timeframe for implementation in *Canada—Pharmaceutical Patents* was much faster than in *Canada—Dairy Products*—see Tables 4.4 and 4.5 for these two disputes' timelines in comparison.[31] This variation can be explained by the affected firms' integration into value chains, which mobilized with

[31] The average time, in months, for Canada to comply with adverse panel rulings is 19 months—by my own calculations. This means that Canada's compliance in *Canada—Pharmaceutical Patents* was significantly faster than usual, while its compliance in response to *Canada—Dairy Products* was significantly slower.

Table 4.5 Overview of Canada—Pharmaceuticals

December 1997	EU requests consultations with Canada over the Canadian patent regulations
March 2000	Canada's stockpiling regulations regarding patented pharmaceuticals found to be WTO-inconsistent Neither party appeals the decision
February 2001	Bill S-17 to bring compliance is introduced in the Canadian parliament
March 2001	Rx&D members request the government to comply Canadian Generic Drug Manufacturers counter-mobilize and ask for non-compliance
June 2001	Bill S-17 is approved by the Canadian House of Commons as well as the Senate after three readings in each chamber

their subsidiaries and affiliates and pressed policymakers to comply with the adverse ruling. A close examination of these two cases thus shows that in the absence of mobilized domestic interest groups in favor of swift implementation, policymakers who face protectionist pressures prolong compliance, and in those cases the complexity of the form of implementation increases the delay in the compliance process. However, even in the face of complexity, WTO Members promptly comply with adverse panel rulings if the affected domestic firms are integrated into value chains, whose mobilization changes the domestic balance of interests in favor of swift implementation.

4.3.1 *Canada's Delayed Compliance with Protectionist Pressures and a Complex Form of Implementation*

On October 8, 1997, the United States, later joined by New Zealand, requested consultations with Canada over its dairy export scheme and its administration of the tariff rate quota on imported milk products. The source of the dispute was the Canadian "special milk class" scheme, which the complainants argued was indirectly subsidizing exporters. This different milk classification system in Canada was the product of the Comprehensive Agreement on Special Class Pooling that was hailed by the Canadian Dairy Commission (CDC) under the National Milk Marketing Plan in response to the Uruguay Agreement in 1995. Canada attempted to replace its old dairy export subsidy scheme by introducing "special milk classes" that classified milk based on its end use put by the processors—e.g., either for domestic consumption or for exporting—and producers whose dairy products destined for exports effectively bought milk at a cheaper price (Cox et al. 2001). The complainants thus argued that Canada indirectly subsidized milk exports and was in violation of several WTO agreements.[32]

After unsuccessful consultations between the parties, the dispute entered the adjudicative phase of the DSM and resulted in a six-year legal battle where Canada delayed complying with the adverse rulings of the panel until mid-2003—after a failed attempt at correcting its illegal export regime in 2001 and two different compliance panels with appeal procedures.[33] Canada's response to litigation was primarily shaped by several domestic actors across Canada who sought protection, including some multinational firms and the Dairy Farmers of Ontario (DFO) and Federation of Milk Producers of Quebec (PLQ), who represented individual firms that accounted for 90% of the affected dairy producers (Verheul 2003). Along with the federal umbrella organization Dairy Farmers of Canada, the state-supported dairy sector was in close cooperation with the Canadian policymakers in complying with the WTO ruling (Krikorian 2005). When the WTO AB upheld the panel ruling that the Canadian measures were indeed violating WTO law in late 1999, PLQ called an extraordinary meeting in Quebec, where some 2000 individual milk producers attended and protested the government's original plan to comply with the ruling by eliminating "special milk classes" (PLQ 2000, 2013). The organization also requested an injunction to suspend the newly proposed regulation in local courts (ibid.).[34] Even though the DFO initially responded to the WTO ruling with indifference, stating that the elimination of export subsidies would only require minimal changes to the supply management system (Veeman 2000), individual farmers

[32] WT/DS103/1. The complainants argued that the Canadian measures were inconsistent with Articles II, X and X1 of the GATT 1994, Articles 3, 4, 8, 9 and 10 of the Agreement on Agriculture, Article 3 of the SCM Agreement, and Articles 1, 2 and 3 of the Import Licensing Agreement.

[33] For the legislative changes Canada attempted throughout the dispute, see USDA (2001) and for Canada's final implementation, see USTR statement. Accessed on February 22, 2017, via: https://ustr.gov/archive/Document_Library/Press_Releases/2003/May/US_Canada_Reach_Agreement_on_Dairy_Exports_to_UShtml.html.

[34] Grant Hargrave and Joanne Pritchard, "Quebec Dairy Farmers Seek Price Stability," *The Militant* 64 (37), October 2, 2000. Accessed on June 15, 2016, via http://www.themilitant.com/2000/6437/643754.shtml.

expressed their fear of losing subsidies.[35] Moreover, agri-food companies that use domestic dairy inputs in their productions, such as McCain Foods, also spoke strongly against changing the program. Their CEO, appearing before the Canadian House of Commons Standing Committee on Foreign Affairs and International Trade, pleaded that Canada keep the program intact, otherwise they would be unable to operate in Canada without the competitively priced domestic dairy inputs they use in their products (Park 1999).

In response, Canadian officials opted to deregulate dairy exports to implement the panel ruling by replacing the "special milk class system" with "commercial export milk" licenses that were issued to producers. The new system practically kept the subsidies in place and was immediately rejected by the complainants who claimed "Canada just re-arranged the chairs on the deck of the Titanic" (Krikorian 2005, p. 936) and even Canadian officials expressed their doubt as to the WTO compliance of the new measures (USDA 2000).

In a surprising turn of events, when Canada appealed the panel ruling—again—the AB ruled in December of 2001 that without more facts, "it was unable to complete the analysis of the claims."[36] In Canada, then-Trade Minister Pierre Pettigrew and Agriculture and Agri-Food Minister Lyle Vanclief claimed this to be a victory due to the "close cooperation with the industry and the provinces" and stated that the ruling "validated" the position of Canada.[37] This blessing in disguise for Canada was short-lived, however, and the second compliance panel requested by the US and New Zealand concluded after the AB ruling that the Canadian system of "commercial export milk" licenses was still inconsistent with WTO law.[38]

[35] Stuart Laidlaw, "On the Path to the Farm Factory," *Toronto Star*, Sunday April 2, 2000.

[36] Appellate Body Report, *Canada—Measures Affecting Dairy Exports*, WT/DS113/AB/RW.

[37] "Canada Welcomes WTO Ruling in Dairy Dispute," Inside U.S. Trade, December 3, 2001. Accessed on May 20, 2016, via: http://insidetrade.com/sites/insidetrade.com/files/documents/pdf3/wto2001_6735.pdf.

[38] Appellate Body Report, *Canada—Measures Affecting Dairy Exports*, WT/DS113/AB/RW2.

In Ontario, the Georgian Bay Company, a politically active large producer of dairy products, directly lobbied different levels of the government and also mobilized some 100 small farmers against compliance.[39] PLQ also gave a direct harsh response to the ruling. The chairman of PLQ criticized the government in the House of Commons Standing Committee hearing on the final WTO ruling, arguing that "the Government of Canada must now make a choice and it must clearly decide whether it wants to protect supply management or whether it wants to abandon one of its production sectors, which would then disappear" (Belzile 2003).

Since this dispute directly involved domestically protected exporters, the political battle that I predicted did not occur. Theoretically, I would have expected import-competing firms and exporters to battle for influence over trade policy. Yet, since there were no import competitors targeted in this dispute, the only actors were domestically protected exporters. Regardless, however, I note that in the absence of domestic actors who sought swift compliance, the pro-protectionist actors were able to exert political influence and delay implementation.

Eventually, however, both Ontario and Quebec, along with the other Canadian provinces, expressed that they would bring their provincial legislation in line with WTO law because the majority of the dairy production was still catered to domestic demand. Department of Foreign Affairs and International Trade made it clear that they would seek an even more flexible timetable for the dairy sector to adjust to the elimination of subsidies (Burney 2003). Finally, in May 2003, Canada complied with the WTO ruling and announced that all subsidies to the dairy sector were to be eliminated and "commercial export milk" licenses were no longer to be issued.

In addition to unfavorable domestic conditions, Canada's delay in compliance was also influenced by the complex form of implementation that was required to bring Canada in line with its WTO commitments.

[39] "Dairy Farmers Battling: Fight for Survival for 100 owners," *The Gazette*, March 24, 2003. Accessed on June 25, 2016, via: http://www.iatp.org/news/dairy-farmers-battling-fight-for-survival-for-100-owners. For the details of the lobbying activity of Georgian Bay Milk Company, see the in-house lobbying report provided by the Office of the Commissioner of Lobbying of Canada. Accessed on June 20, 2016, via: https://lobbycanada.gc.ca/app/secure/ocl/lrs/do/vwRg?cno=2197&regId=502083&lang=eng.

The "special milk classes" scheme was administered by a federal body—the Canadian Dairy Commission–by each province separately. Therefore, invalidating that export subsidy program required separate provincial regulatory changes as well as a federal modification. For Canada's first attempt to comply with the adverse panel ruling in 1999, Quebec, Ontario, Prince Edward Island, New Brunswick, Nova Scotia, Alberta, British Columbia, Manitoba, and Saskatchewan all had to make changes in their provincial legislation (Vinet 2000).[40] This meant that stakeholder meetings, committee meetings, and subcommittee meetings and public consultations needed to be held in each different province. Essentially, compliance with the ruling required all the provinces to bring their own legislation in line with Canada's WTO commitments, and even though the federal Department of Agriculture and Agri-Food Canada "could provide some advice on the broad guidelines, the reality is that the responsibility for developing the actual programs and the responsibility for implementing these programs for export really rested at the provincial level" (Vinet 2000). When federal members of the Parliament asked about the provinces' progress with regard to implementation, the DFAIT director who was also advising the provinces answered: "it all depends on the results of negotiations at the provincial level, and at this point in time we're not in a position to say whether Ontario will be ready before New Brunswick or Quebec before Alberta. It's just not there" (Saint-Jacques 2000).

In sum, the analysis of Canada's response to this dispute helps me verify the hypothesis that WTO Members bring about swift compliance when the affected firms are highly integrated and they press their preferences to bring about trade liberalizing policy change in response to WTO litigation. I showed that complying with the adverse panel ruling in *Canada—Dairy Products* proved to be a difficult task for Canada because the domestic actors in this dispute were primarily pro-protectionist Canadian milk producers that did not engage in value-added trade with foreign enterprises. In the absence of pro-compliance constituencies, the policymakers catered to the demands of protectionist groups that sought to delay compliance. In addition, the form of implementation required to correct the WTO-inconsistent dairy export subsidy regime was a complex one. As a result, Canada delayed complying with the WTO ruling for

[40] See also Canadian Dairy Commission annual report, 2004. Accessed on June 10, 2016, via: http://www.cdc-ccl.gc.ca/CDC/userfiles/file/ENG%202003%202004.pdf.

almost six years, reportedly impairing the US and New Zealand trade up to 70 million USD every year (USDA 2001).

4.3.2 Canada's Swift Implementation in the Face of Complexity

On December 19, 1997, the EU requested consultations with Canada over its 1993 amendment to the Patent Act, which allowed drug manufacturers to avoid conferring rights to patent owners of certain generic pharmaceutical products. The source of the dispute was two provisions in the 1993 amendment. First, the Canadian legislation now allowed generic drug manufacturers to "stockpile" patented pharmaceutical products when they were anticipating the expiration of patents so that they could enter the market with full inventory immediately after the end of the patent term (Gifford 2004).[41] Second, the changes to the Canadian Patent Act also included a provision that allowed generic drug manufacturers to prepare their own submissions for regulatory review during a patent term—the so-called regulatory review provision (Patent Act, 55.2(1), 1993). The EU argued that these two provisions prevented patent protections on products during their full patent terms and thus were violating Articles 27.1, 28, and 33 of the TRIPS Agreement.

The panel ruled in favor of the EU with regard to the stockpiling provision in the Canadian Patent Act but found the regulatory review provision to be in line with the TRIPS Agreement. Neither party appealed the decision, and Canada swiftly complied with the panel ruling by repealing the stockpiling provision via *Bill S-17* on June 14, 2001 within 14 months of the adoption of the panel report.[42] Therefore, even though Canada chose a complex form of implementation to comply with the panel ruling—a legislative action that required three different readings in the Canadian Senate as well as the House of Commons, public hearings, and committee meetings—the procedures proceeded very quickly and there were no delays in implementation.[43]

[41] See also Government of Canada, The Patent Act, R.S. c4. Accessed on August 21, 2016, via: http://www.laws-lois.justice.gc.ca/eng/acts/P-4/.

[42] Government of Canada, Act to Amend the Patent Act (Bill S-17). Accessed August 21, 2016, via: http://laws-lois.justice.gc.ca/eng/annualstatutes/2001_10/page-1.html.

[43] For the legislative history of the bill, see Canadian Parliament Legislative Summaries. Accessed on April 21, 2016, via: http://www.lop.parl.gc.ca/About/Parliament/LegislativeSummaries/bills_ls.asp?ls=S17&Parl=37&Ses=1. It is important to note that this

The reason why Canada was able to quickly comply with the panel's recommendation in this dispute was because the targeted measure involved Canadian pharmaceutical manufacturers that were dependent on imports from abroad, which mobilized and lobbied the Canadian government to comply with the panel ruling. In the year 2000, overseas imports accounted for 75% of the Canadian domestic pharmaceutical market—most of which consisted of chemicals used in the production of pharmaceutical products (Lexchin 2001). The domestic pharmaceutical sector in Canada mainly consisted at the time of subsidiaries and affiliates of primarily research-based multinational companies, which provided billions of dollars in investment to the Canadian economy (Gifford 2004), such as GlaxoSmithKline, Bayer, and Novartis. These companies rallied behind the association of Canadian Research Based Pharmaceutical Companies (Rx&D)—which is now known as "Innovative Medicines Canada"—and fully supported *Bill S-17* in order to comply with the WTO ruling. The pharmaceutical lobby was already known to have supported several high-ranking members of the government, including the Deputy Prime Minister John Manley, mostly through donations to their campaigns (Lexchin 2005). Therefore, their influence in the Canadian government was quite accepted. Unsurprisingly, they were engaged in direct lobbying for the successful enactment of several pieces of legislation, including *Bill S-17*, that benefited patent holders with a large lobbying team that included the former advisor to the Canadian deputy prime minister (Lobby Canada 2001). During the Proceedings of the Standing Senate Committee on Banking, Trade and Commerce, Rx&D and members demanded that the government comply with the ruling by taking "rapid steps to correct" the WTO-inconsistent measure (Baumgartner 2001). The association argued that it was "the right thing to do to increase the research-based pharmaceutical industry's international competitiveness ... and the first step in advancing the government's innovation agenda" (ibid.). Such appeals to the "innovative" nature of the pharmaceutical industry were clearly linked with Rx&D's investment promises, and the continuing investment into research was conditional upon the political climate in Canada. Indeed, the members of the association had previously kept their promise of a substantial increase to

particular legislation also amended some other provisions in the Canadian Patent Act in response to the US challenge in *Canada—Patent Protection*.

their investment, amounting to some 500 million USD (Jordan 2005, p. 44), as long as patents remained protected in Canada. Therefore, these international firms exercised a strong pull on the direction of policy because they were bringing employment, investment, and they directly contributed to the politicians' campaigns. Thus, when a dispute touched upon the interests of these firms, their mobilization was followed by a very quick response from the Canadian government, which catered to their demands without delay.

In response, the Canadian Generic Drug Manufacturers Association (CDMA) engaged in counter lobbying but met with no success. The organization was already quite small in size and in capital, as opposed to Rx&D, and although the president of the organization warned that *Bill S-17* "contributes to the steadily worsening legal and regulatory environment for generic drugs in Canada" (Keon 2001), the bill met surprisingly little opposition from different factions within the Canadian legislature. Despite requiring three different readings in the Senate and the House of Commons, with different subcommittee meetings, *Bill S-17* passed within four months of its introduction. A similar account describes the legislative process of the above-mentioned *Bill C-17*—a bill that provided extra protection to patented pharmaceuticals in Canada—it was a statutory act that was fast tracked by Ottawa senators whose political livelihood benefited greatly from international pharmaceutical companies.

It should be noted that in this particular dispute the role of exporters was noticeably absent. In line with my expectations, exporters should have mobilized to avoid potential retaliatory sanctions and their mobilization in combination with highly international pharmaceutical companies should have changed the domestic constellation of interests in favor of compliance. Yet, I have not been able to trace the role of exporters anywhere in response to this dispute. That being said, even without the explicit threat of retaliation, the implicit (potential) retaliation, which is inherent in any WTO dispute (Bown 2009, p. 131) played an important role in inducing compliance; as the Minister of Industry clearly announced that by complying with the ruling Canada could "avoid unnecessary retaliatory measures" from its trade partners.[44]

[44] Inside US Trade, March 22, 2001 "New Canadian Patent Act Aims for WTO Compliance." Accessed on April 2, 2017, via: https://insidetrade.com/content/new-canadian-patent-act-aims-wto-compliance.

Consequently, I am able to confirm the hypothesis that firms' that mobilize and press for their preferences shape WTO Members' responses to litigation. However, even without exporters explicitly mobilizing for swift compliance, policymakers seem to take potential retaliation into account and act accordingly. I demonstrated that Canada's response to the adverse panel ruling in *Canada—Pharmaceutical Patents* was shaped by the interests of the mobilized pharmaceutical firms, which greatly favored compliance. These import-dependent firms entered into a coalition with other international firms that shared their interests in accessing cheaper imports and protecting patented products. With the domestic conditions conducive to compliance, the Canadian policymakers swiftly implemented the WTO panel's decision even in the face of legal complexity.

References

American Consumers for Affordable Homes. 2003. Treatment of Sector 201 Duties and Countervailing Duties, statement released on October 9, 2003. Available at http://enforcement.trade.gov/download/canada-softwood-lumber/acah-softwood-lumber-cmts.pdf. Accessed on March 21.

Baumgartner, Aldo. 2001. Statement on the Amendment of the Patent Act. Speech, Ottawa. *Proceedings of the Standing Senate Committee on Banking, Trade and Commerce*, Canadian Senate, March 21.

Belzile, A. 2003. *Statement on the World Trade Organization's Decision on the Canadian Dairy Export Policy*. Speech, Proceedings of the Standing Committee on Agriculture and AgriFood, 18 March, Ottowa.

Bown, C. 2009. *Self-Enforcing Trade: Developing Countries and WTO Dispute Settlement*. Washington: Brookings Institution Press.

Briggs, J., S. Laaksonen-Craig, K. Niquidet, and C. van Kooten. 2005. Resolving Canada-U.S. Trade Disputes in Agriculture and Forestry: Lessons from Lumber. Resource Economics and Policy Analysis Research Group Working Paper 2005-03. University of Victoria.

Burney, I. 2003. *Statement on the World Trade Organization's Decision on the Canadian Dairy Export Policy*. Speech, Proceedings of the Standing Committee on Agriculture and AgriFood, 18 March, Ottowa.

Bush, G. 2002. Announcement on the Temporary Safeguards for the Steel Industry. United States White House Office of the Press Secretary. Available at https://georgewbush-whitehouse.archives.gov/infocus/steel/.

Charron, M. 2005. Lumber I to IV. History of the Canada—U.S. Softwood Lumber Dispute. Canadian Parliamentary Research Service report TIPS-134E published on December 19.

Consuming Industries Trade Action Coalition. 2002. Statement 'Tariff Exclusion Process Will Not Solve Steel Consumers' Struggles, December 4.

Cox, T., D. Le Roy, and E. Goddard. 2001. Dairy Disputes in North America: A Case Study. In *Trade Liberalization under NAFTA: Report Card on Agriculture, Proceedings of the Sixth Agricultural and Food Policy Systems Information Workshop*, ed. R.M.A. Loyns, K. Meilke, R.D. Knutson, and A. Yunez-Naude, 253–282. San Diego. March 2000.

Fergusson, I. 2011. United States-Canada Trade and Economic Relationship: Prospects and Challenges. U.S. Congressional Research Service report RL33087. Available at https://fas.org/sgp/crs/row/RL33087.pdf. Accessed on March 2 2016.

Francois, J., and L. Baughman. 2001. Estimated Economic Effects of Proposed Import Relief Remedies for Steel. Report Prepared by Trade Partnership Worldwide LLC. Available at http://tradepartnership.com/reports/estimated-economic-effects-of-proposed-import-relief-remedies-for-steel-2001/.

Greenspan, Alan. 2003. Speech Given at the "Economic Outlook" Hearing Before the Joint Economic Committee of the United States Congress, May 21.

Gifford, D. 2004. *Government Policy Towards Innovation in the United States, Canada, and the European Union as Manifested in Patent, Copyright, and Competition Laws*. University of Minnesota Law School SMU Law Review paper 1339 (2004). Available at http://scholarship.law.umn.edu/faculty_articles/333. Accessed on June 20, 2020.

Jacobs, M. 2016. Smart Threats and Success in WTO Dispute Settlement: The Bush Steel Tariffs. E-International Relations, March 24, 2016. Available at http://www.e-ir.info/2016/03/24/smart-threats-and-success-in-wto-dispute-settlement-the-bush-steel-tariffs/. Accessed on June 20, 2020.

Jordan, M. 2005. *The Politics of Drug Patenting in Canada*. Masters dissertation, University of Saskatchewan.

Keon, J. 2001. *Statement on the amendment of the Patent Act*. Speech, House of Commons Standing Committee on Industry, Science, and Technology, 17 May, Ottowa.

Krikorian, J. 2005. Planes, Trains and Automobiles: The Impact of the WTO "Court" on Canada in Its First Ten Years. *Journal of International Economic Law* 8 (4): 921–975.

Leuiliette, Timothy. 2003. Impact of the Section 201 Safeguard Action on Certain Steel Products. Speech given before the U.S. House of Representatives Committee on Ways and Means Subcommittee on Trade, March 26.

Lexchin, J. 2001. Globalization, Trade Deals, and Drugs: Heads the Industry Wins Tails Canada Loses. *Canada Centre for Policy Alternatives Briefing Paper* 2 (8). November 2001.

Lexchin, J. 2005. Intellectual Property Rights and the Canadian Pharmaceutical Marketplace: Where Do We Go From Here? *International Journal of Health Service* 35 (2): 237–256.

Lobby Canada. 2001. *Registration and Organization Information: Rx&D*. Office of the Commissioner of Lobbying of Canada. Available at https://lobbycanada.gc.ca/app/secure/ocl/lrs/do/vwRg?cno=12328®Id=491884#regStart. Accessed on June 20, 2020.

Mavroidis, Petros. 2000. Remedies in the WTO Legal System: Between a Rock and a Hard Place. *European Journal of International Law* 11 (4): 763–813.

Park, A. 1999. *Examination of Canada's Trade Objectives and the Forthcoming Agenda of the World Trade Organization (WTO)*. Speech, Proceedings of the Standing Committee on Foreign Affairs and International Trade, 25 March, New Brunswick.

Pauwelyn, Joost. 2000. Enforcement and Countermeasures in the WTO: Rules are Rules-Toward a More Collective Approach. *American Journal of International Law* 94 (2): 335–347.

Producteurs de lait du Québec (PLQ). 2000. *Annual Report: Training and Information*, On file with author.

Producteurs de lait du Québec (PLQ). 2013. *2013 Annual Report: 30 Years, Proud of Our Collective Achievements*, On file with author.

Przeworski, A., and H. Teune. 1970. *The Logic of Comparative Social Inquiry*. New York: Wiley.

Read, R. 2005. The EU-US WTO Steel Dispute: Political Economy of Protection and the Efficacy of the WTO Dispute Settlement Understanding. In *The WTO and the Regulation of International Trade: Recent Trade Disputes Between the European Union and the United States*, ed. Nicholas Perdikis and Robert Read, 135–175. Cheltenham: Edward Elgar.

Reif, L. 2007. Desperate Softwood Lumber Companies? The Canada-US Softwood Lumber Dispute and NAFTA Chapter 11. *Alberta Law Review* 45 (2): 357–380.

Rus, T. 2007. The Short, Unhappy life of the Byrd Amendment, N.Y.U. *Journal of Legislation and Public Policy* 10 (2): 427–443.

Saint-Jacques, J. 2000. *Information Session on the Canadian Dairy Exports under the World Trade Organization (WTO)*. Speech, Proceedings of the Standing Committee on Agriculture and AgriFood, 24 February, Ottowa.

United States Coalition for Fair Lumber Imports (USLC). 2002a. WTO: Canadian Subsidies Exist, Subsidy to be Recalculated. Statement released on September 27.

United States Coalition for Fair Lumber Imports (USLC). 2002b. U.S. Lumber Industry Seeks Negotiated Offset to Unfair Trade. Statement released on December 17.

United States Coalition for Fair Lumber Imports (USLC). 2003. Canadian Lumber Proposal Warrants Further Discussion. Statement released on July 31.

United States Department of Agriculture (USDA). 2000. *Canadian Dairy Industry Spokesman Speculates New Dairy Regime Won't Be WTO Compliant.* Global Agricultural Information Network Report CA0124, August 2000, On file with author.

United States Department of Agriculture (USDA). 2001. *Canada's Subsidized Dairy Exports: The Issue of WTO Compliance.* Special article prepared by Economic Research Service, August 2001, On file with author.

United States International Trade Commission (USITC). 2001. Determinations Concerning Impact of Imports of Steel on U.S. Industry, October 23. https://www.usitc.gov/press_room/news_release/2001/er1023y1.pdf.

United States International Trade Commission (USITC). 2003. Steel-Consuming Industries: Competitive Conditions With Respect to Steel Safeguard Measures (Investigation No. 332–452).

Veeman, M. 2000. Preparing for the Challenges and Opportunities Beyond 2000 Through Future Dairy Policy in Canada: Implications for Production and Trade. *Advances in Dairy Technology* 12: 331–341.

Verheul, S. 2003. *Statement on the World Trade Organization's Decision on the Canadian Dairy Export Policy.* Speech, Proceedings of the Standing Committee on Agriculture and AgriFood, 18 March, Ottawa.

Vinet, S. 2000. *Information Session on the Canadian Dairy Exports under the World Trade Organization (WTO).* Speech, Proceedings of the Standing Committee on Agriculture and AgriFood, 24 February, Ottawa.

Wilson, B. 2007. Compliance by WTO Members with Adverse WTO Dispute Settlement Rulings: The Record to Date. *Journal of International Economic Law* 10 (2): 397–403.

Zhang, D. 2007. *The Softwood Lumber War. Politics, Economics, and the Long U.S.-Canadian Trade. Dispute.* New York: Routledge.

Zhang, Daowei, and David Laband. 2003. From Senators to the President: Solve the Lumber Problem or Else. *Public Choice* 123 (3): 393–410.

Zoellick, R. 2003. Press Briefing by US Trade Representative Zoellick on Ending the Temporary Steel Safeguards. Washington: The White House Office of the Press Secretary. Available at http://iipdigital.usembassy.gov/st/english/texttrans/2003/12/20031204164450yessedo0.718197.html#ixzz45cv7YfiB. Accessed on April 12, 2016.

CHAPTER 5

Conclusion

Abstract This chapter outlines the main findings of the book and proposes further research avenues. In doing so, it also provides an overview of the implications of its findings for trade politics in general, especially considering the growing economic nationalist rhetoric that have led to rising trade tensions across the globe. The primary finding of the book is that value chains shape preferences of firms and sectors toward open trade policies. This can be observed at the WTO dispute settlement and in response to WTO litigation, through which organized interests have mobilized for swift compliance with the rulings of the WTO panels. Moreover, we can observe such international firms' and sectors' mobilization beyond the WTO and opposing trade-restrictive measures enacted in the context of trade tensions across the globe. These observations indicate that even without a fully functioning WTO dispute settlement mechanism, there may be less to worry about backtracking an open world economy.

Keywords Trade politics · International institutions · Value chains

A. B. Yildirim, *Value Chains and WTO Disputes*,
https://doi.org/10.1007/978-3-030-49094-2_5

5.1 Main Findings and the Contributions

In this book, I analyzed the international political economy of WTO dispute settlement. I investigated the political and economic sources of (non-)compliance with adverse panel rulings in nearly all WTO disputes between 1995 and 2016 using alternative sources of data and alternative analytical methods that are particularly suited for my research question. I proposed that when defendants at the WTO face litigation affecting firms and sectors that are highly integrated into value chains, the pro-compliance preferences of these actors lead governments to comply more quickly. This is because such disputes bring about the political mobilization of a coalition of domestic groups favoring compliance, composed of highly integrated firms and sectors wishing to access cheaper imports, joined by exporters seeking to avoid the imposition of retaliatory measures.

To test the validity of my theoretical expectations, I first conducted a survival analysis using Cox proportional hazard modeling, which revealed that the defendant WTO Members' propensity to comply with adverse rulings in WTO DSM is indeed crucially affected by the level of integration of the targeted sector. My findings suggest that defendants WTO Members are faster in bringing about trade-liberalizing domestic policy change in the face of adverse panel rulings at the WTO DSM and overcome the domestic resistance to compliance when affected sectors are more heavily integrated into value chains. The marginal effect of integration seems to be greatest at low-to-moderate levels, perhaps because relatively small levels of integration are needed to convince domestic groups to mobilize, and there are simply fewer non-mobilized groups available at higher levels. Furthermore, by using different proxies for integration, I demonstrated that my results are not driven by my modeling choices.

From my large-n analysis, I selected two cases for in-depth examination involving process tracing. I chose the responses of the US and Canada to litigation and compared their behavior in four different disputes that revealed the dynamics of firm activity in response to WTO disputes. I showed through my cases that affected firms in defendant economies lobby for swift compliance and press their preferences to policymakers throughout the course of a dispute and especially after an adverse panel ruling is rendered by the WTO panels. I demonstrated that firms enter into coalitions and lobby single-handedly to achieve their policy objectives. Moreover, my case studies showed that the complexity of the form of implementation chosen by the defendant WTO Members does not decisively lead to swifter compliance. Quite the opposite, even in the face of complexity, defendant WTO Member fast track policy change when the domestic conditions are conducive to this outcome—i.e., highly integrated firms' politically mobilize.

My findings have important implications not only for the study of trade policy and the politics of WTO dispute settlement, but also for the analysis of the conditions that make international institutions effective more broadly. First, I support existing studies that stress that the politics of trade policy can no longer be exclusively conceived of as a conflict pitting producers wishing to increase market access opportunities abroad against producers seeking protection from foreign competition in the domestic market. The internationalization of trade, production, and distribution systems has changed the nature of the political conflict that underlies the making of trade policy, leading to the emergence of firms integrated into value chains as a key set of actors that is affected by and mobilizes over trade policies. This book thus contributes to our understanding of the politics of trade policy by highlighting how the judicial institutions of the WTO affect the preferences and patterns of mobilization of this important set of trade-related interests, and how such dynamics contribute to particular trade policy outcomes.

Second, my findings broaden our understanding of the political implications of the growing internationalization of production in the world economy. While the potential for such processes to make trade liberalization easier to achieve has already been widely noted (Antràs and Staiger 2012; Chase 2003),[1] no study so far has systematically assessed how different patterns of integration into value chains can affect compliance at the WTO. I therefore contribute to this strand of literature by showing how growing internationalization of production processes in the world economy facilitate international trade liberalization by creating political conditions that strengthen the WTO's capacity to enforce multilateral trade rules. This is a particularly important finding given that the growing inability of the WTO to perform its legislative function—sustaining the liberalization of world trade through the adoption of broad multilateral

[1] See also, Orefice and Rocha (2014), Eckhardt (2015), Eckhardt and Poletti (2016), Jensen et al. (2015), Kim (2015), Manger (2009), and Milner (1987).

trade deals—is contributing to its judicial institutions becoming central to the organization's political system (Goldstein and Steinberg 2008).

Finally, and more generally, this book contributes to the literature on international cooperation by advancing our knowledge of the micro-foundations of states' cooperative behavior in international trade relations. I reiterate the simple but crucial point that international cooperation is sustained by institutions much more stably when domestic actors' preferences converge with the preferences of member states and their representatives in international fora. This result speaks to the neoliberal institutional school of thought, which highlights the importance of institutions in light of actor preferences in different levels of governance and the interplay between the domestic and international policymaking fields.

Additionally, my argument and empirical findings suggest several avenues for further research and bring at least two policy implications. First, the reform of the dispute settlement mechanism that materialized with the creation of the WTO was meant to increase both first and second-order compliance with WTO rules (Von Stein 2012). While this book has shown that integration into value chains can increase the likelihood that WTO enforcement institutions will be effective in fostering second-order compliance, it remains an open question whether similar dynamics affect first-order compliance. Does integration make the imposition of protectionist trade policies or measures less likely in the very first place? Many previous studies have shown that trading nations have resorted to protectionism to a lesser degree than might have been expected in the wake of the global financial crisis that erupted in 2007–2008. While the presence of credible enforcement mechanisms such as the WTO DSM certainly played a significant role in constraining such protectionist demands across the board, logic suggests that the effectiveness of enforcement institutions in fostering first-order compliance should be more pronounced whenever trading partners are heavily integrated into value chains (Baccini and Kim 2012; Kim 2012). My evidence shows that WTO-incompatible trade barriers do indeed get erected in sectors with very high integration into value chains. This might suggest that, from a domestic political standpoint, policymakers still enact potentially WTO-incompatible, disruptive trade policies whose benefits outweigh their costs—at least in the short term until they are targeted through inter-state litigation. However, because a rigorous analysis of value chains' implications for first-order compliance is beyond the scope of this study, I suggest that further research could investigate more systematically whether, and eventually how, these structural transformations in the world economy systematically affect first-order compliance with multilateral trade rules.

Second, the increasingly important phenomenon of the internationalization of production is not limited to how value chains affect first and second-order compliance at the WTO. In addition to offering the institutional means to enforce trade rules, the multilateral trading system should perform a legislative function. An important question in the analysis of the effects of value chain integration is, therefore, how this integration affects preferences and patterns of mobilization of trade-related interests in multilateral trade negotiations. While some scholars argue that value chains create powerful incentives for trading nations to engage in trade liberalization via PTAs, others have shown that import-dependent firms have played a key role in pushing powerful WTO Members to support far-reaching trade liberalization commitments in the Doha Round (Baldwin 2014; Poletti and De Bièvre 2016). Further research should tackle both of these important questions if we are to understand how the changing character of international trade will affect the stability of the multilateral trading system. Given current tensions and on-going multilateral negotiations to sustain a global institutional framework, understanding patterns of domestic actors' mobilization is ever more significant.

What my research can also inform is that it would be worthwhile to think about introducing financial remedies in cases of continuous non-compliance. My findings suggest very clearly that WTO Members actively engage in delay tactics regarding compliance—a point recognized by scholars in the field (Zimmermann 2006; Shoyer et al. 2005). This means the window of opportunism can be slightly tightened without legalizing the DSU much further. Resonating with other scholars' views on the potential positive effects of financial remedies (e.g., Bronckers and Baetens 2013), when a member actively refuses to comply after its wrongdoing is ascertained, financial remedies can be appropriated as restitution. This would apply to the time frame during which the member is refusing to implement a panel ruling in good faith—perhaps starting the clock after the DSB–mandated 15 months has passed. Policymakers' calculus would thus include damages not only when retaliation is granted, but also when they actively engage in delay tactics to appease their domestic constituencies. I believe this should decrease the time until defendants bring forth compliance and help avoid foot dragging.

Such changes to the DSU would require unanimous consent of the WTO membership and while I believe this would be feasible in the long term, current political dynamics may not be too conducive to change. However, if an opportunity is presented with a reformed dispute settlement system, an option could be to use financial remedies as an alternative to retaliation, then once it is seen (if it is seen) as a viable alternative, then the change would be much more feasible. From the perspective of the most active, the largest WTO Members—i.e., the EU and the US—I actually think such gradual change might be welcome, considering how much they litigate themselves and also acquiesce to authorized retaliation. For the smaller WTO Members, the change would be especially welcome since they have limited resources to impose retaliatory sanctions that induce compliance behavior from their larger counterparts.

In addition, from a broad trade policy perspective, I suggest governments take into account the growing relevance of firms active in value chains. My results suggest that policymakers who respond to the demands of the domestic actors are only concerned with the well-being of these firms *ex-post* to the erection of trade barriers. Yet, their growing relevance cannot be ignored and put on hold unless they are aggrieved and looking for remedies. Policymakers should be able to assess the use of protectionist policies (may they be WTO-compatible or not) by taking into account the implications of trade restrictions on firms who rely on imports, intermediate products, and value-added goods and services in general.

5.2 Twenty-First-Century Trade Tensions in the Context of Value Chains

As I noted in the introduction, the arguments made in this book comes at a time where trade tensions have been garnering increasing traction. While it would be futile to try to delve into the causes and consequences of such tensions that evolve on a daily basis, three broad points can be made in relation to the findings I highlight in this book.

The first on is on the so-called backlash against globalization. Indeed, both policymakers and academics alike agree that the turn of the century has led to a growing discontent over what is broadly termed "globalization"—covering many dimensions ranging from immigration policies to the function of post-Breton Woods economic institutions that attempt to sustain a rather neoliberal economic order. A long line of research has been attempting to understand this backlash and the debate over the distributional consequences of globalization (Baccini et al. 2018; Ruggie 1982; Katzenstein 1985; Rodrik 1998).

The findings of this book speak to this literature by noting that there is actually quite high support for free trade policies and a strong coalition of firms and sectors in favor of international trade. In the context of the WTO, I show that internationalization and cross border value chains reinforces private actors' preferences over open trade. The implication of this observation highlights that while politics of trade is complex, multifaceted, and increasingly contested, there remains a strong support for an open world economy. Indeed, this finding is in line with studies that show quite high support for international trade by individuals in many advanced and emerging economies.[2] Therefore, one can postulate that grievances of individuals and stakeholders over the complex effects of globalization do not necessarily reflect on international trade per se. This means further research should tackle the crucial question of what attitudes on free trade mean for open borders and globalization in general—especially with regard to policies beyond trade, such as security and immigration.

This relates to the second point about the on-going difficulties facing the World Trade Organization vis-à-vis the findings shown in this book. During the finishing phase of my research, the WTO Appellate Body was crippled by the US Administration's refusal to appoint Appellate Body members with the AB's future uncertain (see Pauwelyn 2019). As the WTO faces important questions about its possible reform and growing skepticism about the institution's ability to fulfill its mission to sustain a rules-based open and free global economy, the implications of my book are somewhat complex. On the one hand, I show that compliance at the WTO DSM is often quite lengthy, which has distributive consequences for domestic actors that are affected by a dispute. One could put forward that delays in compliance frustrate domestic actors' ability to benefit from the dispute settlement system. In turn, mobilizing in favor of the WTO system itself might not be at the top of domestic organized interests' agenda. This could be why we have not seen an orchestrated mobilization from private actors about the importance of WTO DSM. However, this is pure conjecture as there is virtually no research, to the best of my

[2] See, Christian Bluth, A Safety Net to Foster Support for Trade and Globalisation, International Survey on Attitudes towards Trade and Globalisation, *Bertelsmann Stiftung*. Available via: https://ged-project.de/globalization/a-safety-net-to-foster-support-for-trade-and-globalisation/. Accessed on 20 June 2020.

knowledge, that examines firms' and sectors' political mobilization over recent discussion on WTO reform. Further research will benefit greatly from such endeavors.

On the other hand, what my research can shed light is that even without the WTO dispute settlement, many firms' preferences remain the same, i.e., keep trade barriers down. Firms and sectors active along value chains have been mobilizing not only at the WTO DSM but beyond the WTO over trade policies that affect their operations. One can thus postulate that perhaps the demise of the WTO DSM will not necessarily lead to high number of trade barriers. Instead, we have reasons to expect the domestic balance of interests (over trade policies) to remain similar even without a functioning WTO DSM, which can keep the protectionist temptation in check.

This point relates to the third important implication of my findings, i.e., the mobilization of firms and sectors against trade restrictive policies beyond the WTO. The rhetoric and increasingly protectionist trade policy initiatives of the Trump administration against US trade partners are among the most visible examples of the on-going trade tensions between major world economies. In line with my theoretical propositions, value chain actors' mobilization over such policy initiatives (beyond the WTO) is easily observable. The logic I postulate about firms' trade policy preferences and their internationalization would mean that such firms should be mobilizing in favor of open trade in these cases and there is indeed evidence of this.

Firm and sector lobbying activities indicate an orchestrated aggressive push against trade-restricting measures enacted by the Trump administration. Companies that rely on foreign products for their production has been actively engaging in lobbying to either halt the escalation of disputes, or to receive exemptions.[3] This type of individual level lobbying is of course only part of the story. Import-dependent firms, especially retailers, have been extremely active on mobilizing in favor of removing Trump administration's trade barriers and have been able to create a coalition

[3] See, for instance, Levine and Meyer, "Lobbyists Rake in Cash But Can't Kill Trump Tariffs," *Politico*, 6 May, 2018. Accessed on January 29, 2020 via: https://www.politico.com/story/2018/06/05/lobbyists-tariffs-trump-strategy-618926. Regarding retailers' lobbying, see Alex Gangitano, "Top U.S. Retail Companies Urge White House Against More Tariffs on China," *The Hill*, 13 June, 2019. Accessed on January 29, 2020 via: https://thehill.com/business-a-lobbying/448462-top-us-retail-companies-urge-white-house-against-more-tariffs-on-china.

organization. Americans for Free Trade—a massive anti-tariff umbrella organization—that has been lobbying the White House to push back against trade barriers imposed on products entering the US.[4] The overall trend in lobbying is also telling. In 2016, the number of organizations lobbying on tariffs was 76, which more than doubled in the following 2 years and reached around 200 in 2018 and 2019.[5] This is testament to lobbying efforts of free-traders and counter lobbying from groups that benefit from enacted barriers during the same time.

Have import dependent companies and groups been successful in their mobilization? It is too difficult to tell. There are some indications that they are—e.g., the so-called Phase One of China—US Trade Pact for instance. However, by the time this book is published, developments will have taken place and we will have a clearer idea on the success of pro-trade groups that rely on foreign products for their production or revenue in general. One thing is for certain though, in a world characterized by complex production networks and value chains that cross (often several) boundaries, scholars, policymakers, students of international politics and trade, as well as the public in general should re-evaluate assumptions about trade policy and economic relations in general from the perspective of domestic organized interests.

References

Antràs, Pol, and Robert W. Staiger. 2012. Offshoring and the Role of Trade Agreements. *American Economic Review* 102 (7): 3140–3183.

Baccini, L., and H.Y. Kim. 2012. Preventing Protectionism: International Institutions and Trade Policy. *The Review of International Organizations* 7 (4): 369–398.

Baccini, L., Pablo P., and S. Weymouth. 2018. The Distributional Consequences of Preferential Trade Liberalization: Firm-Level Evidence. *International Organization* 71 (2): 373–395.

Baldwin, R. 2014. WTO 2.0: Governance of 21st Century Trade. *The Review of International Organizations* 9 (2): 261–283.

[4] See, Americans for Free Trade 2019, Letter to President Trump. Accessed on January 29, 2020, via: http://americansforfreetrade.com/wp-content/uploads/2019/04/AFT-Final-China-Deal-Letter-to-President-Trump-042219-Final.pdf.

[5] See, for instance, Center for Responsive Politics 2019, *Lobbying Issue Profile: Tariffs*. Accessed on January 29, 2020, via: https://www.opensecrets.org/federal-lobbying/issues/summary?cycle=2019&id=TRF.

Bronckers, M., and F. Baetens. 2013. Reconsidering Financial Remedies in WTO Dispute Settlement. *Journal of International Economic Law* 16 (2): 281–311.
Chase, K. 2003. Economic Interests and Regional Trading Arrangements: The Case of NAFTA. *International Organization* 57 (1): 137–174.
Eckhardt, J. 2015. *Business Lobbying and Trade Governance: The Case of EU-China Relations*. New York and Basingstoke: Palgrave Macmillan.
Eckhardt, J., and A. Poletti. 2016. The Politics of Global Value Chains: Import Dependent Firms and EU-Asia Trade Agreements. *Journal of European Public Policy*. https://doi.org/10.1080/13501763.2015.1085073.
Goldstein, J., and R. Steinberg. 2008. Negotiate or Litigate? Effects of WTO Judicial Delegation on US Trade Politics. *Law and Contemporary Problems* 71 (1): 257–282.
Jensen, B., D. Quinn, and S. Weymouth. 2015. The Influence of Firm Global Supply Chains and Foreign Currency Undervaluations on US Trade Disputes. *International Organization* 69: 913–947.
Katzenstein, P.J. 1985. *Small States in World Markets: Industrial Policy in Europe*. Cornell Studies in Political Economy. Ithaca, NY: Cornell University Press.
Kim, S.Y. 2012. Protectionism During Recession: Is This Time Different? *The Political Economist* 9 (2): 6–8.
Kim, S.Y. 2015. Regionalization in Search of Regionalism: Production Networks and Deep Integration Commitments in Asia's PTAs. In *The Purpose, Design, and Effects of Preferential Trade Agreements*, ed. Andreas Dür and Manfred Elsig. Cambridge: Cambridge University Press.
Manger, Mark. 2009. *Investing in Protection: The Politics of Preferential Trade Agreements Between North and South*. Cambridge: Cambridge University Press.
Milner, H. 1987. Resisting the Protectionist Temptation: Industry and the Making of Trade Policy in France and the United States During the 1970s. *International Organization* 41 (4): 639–665.
Orefice, G., and N. Rocha. 2014. Deep Integration and Production Networks: An Empirical Analysis. *The World Economy* 37 (1): 106–136.
Pauwelyn, Joost. 2019. WTO Dispute Settlement System Post-2019: What to Expect? *Journal of International Economic Law* 22 (3): 297–321. Available at https://doi.org/10.1093/jiel/jgz024.
Poletti, A., and D. De Bièvre. 2016. *Judicial Politics and International Cooperation: From Disputes to Deal-Making at the World Trade Organization*. Colchester: ECPR Press.
Rodrik, D. 1998. Why Do More Open Economies Have Bigger Governments? *Journal of Political Economy* 106 (5): 997–1032.
Ruggie, John Gerard. 1982. International Regimes, Transactions, and Change: Embedded Liberalism in Postwar Economic Order. *International Organization* 36 (2): 379–415.

Shoyer, A., E. Solovy, and A. Koff. 2005. Implementation and Enforcement of Dispute Settlement Decisions. In *The World Trade Organization: Legal, Economic and Political Analysis*, ed. M. Plummer and A. Appleton. New York, NY: Springer.

Von Stein, J. 2012. The Engines of Compliance. In *Synthesizing Insights from International Law and International Relations*, ed. Jeffrey Dunoff and Mark Pollack. Cambridge: Cambridge University Press.

Zimmermann, T. 2006. Negotiating the Review of the World Trade Organization Dispute Settlement Understanding. Cameron May.

Appendix A: Supplementary Analysis for Cox Regression

In this appendix, I provide supplementary information using the TiVA data, given the additional measures I used to operationalize my variable of interest, matching Table 5 in the first analytical chapter, the universe of cases I studied, policies that brought compliance in response to disputes, the operationalization of compliance, and the coding of the European Union with regard to Political Constraints dataset.

In addition, I provide a robustness check for my analysis. I provide an alternative measure of my dependent variable (measuring time from first panel's report, rather than time from the circulation of the final panel's report) and demonstrate that my results are not a result of my measurement choices.

Measuring Time to Compliance and Power Asymmetry

In my primary analysis, I examine time to compliance using the date of the circulation of the AB's ruling as the point of departure. However, in many cases, import-dependent firms may behave strategically, acting on expectations about the panel's ruling, and mobilizing earlier in the process. Thus, I create an alternative measure of the dependent variable, which calculates the time from the first panel ruling that took place, rather than the last point of legal juncture that clarified (non)compliance, and include it in the specifications presented in the main text.

A. B. Yildirim, *Value Chains and WTO Disputes*,
https://doi.org/10.1007/978-3-030-49094-2

Moreover, I also include two alternatives to measure power differences between WTO members in addition to export dependence measure I used in the main analysis. First, I look at the differences in GDP as a crude measure of power imbalance and secondly the defendants' foreign direct investment in the complainant. I provide the results from the analysis using these two measurements in lieu of export dependence.

The results in Table A.1 are consistent with those in Table 5 of the main text. The most notable difference I draw from the results is that the three specifications of the GVC integration measure are significant across all the models except in one where I include foreign direct investment dependence of WTO members. In other words, I observe that foreign value added of sector exports is not a significant factor that shortens compliance when taking into account litigants' FDI dependence. The presence of veto players and a trade barrier's complexity are similarly important, suggesting that these factors play a particularly important role in the dispute settlement process. With respect to my variables of interest, I find results that are substantively similar to those in my main analysis. Each measure of value chain integration is significant, and the magnitude of the coefficients (directly interpretable, given the linear nature of the Cox model) is similar to those in the original analysis. This suggests that my results were not driven by my measurement choices for the dependent variable (Table A.1) or the variable that captures power relations between WTO members (Table A.2).

Table A.1 Results from alternative specification of the dependent variable

	Baseline & time included	*Sector GVC included*	*Sector GVC included*	*Sector GVC included*	*Sector GVC included*	*Sector GVC included*	*Sector GVC included*	*Sector GVC included*	*Sector GVC included*	*Sector GVC included*
Power asymmetry	0.05 (0.10)	0.01 (0.10)	−0.02 (0.10)	−0.02 (0.11)						
FDI share					−0.01 (0.01)	−0.01 (0.01)	−0.01 (0.01)			
Export dependence								−0.01 (0.01)	−0.01 (0.01)	−0.01 (0.01)
Def. Democracy	0.07 (0.05)	0.09 (0.0[illegible])	0.08 (0.05)	0.05 (0.07)	0.10 (0.07)	0.09 (0.07)	0.09 (0.07)	0.11* (0.06)	0.10* (0.06)	0.12* (0.06)
Issue complexity	0.83** (0.24)	0.95*** (0.2[illegible])	0.91*** (0.24)	1.09*** (0.24)	0.86*** (0.25)	0.82*** (0.25)	0.72*** (0.25)	0.89*** (0.25)	0.85*** (0.24)	0.75** (0.24)
Sectoral value added	−0.18* (0.09)	−0.[illegible]8* (0.1[illegible])	−0.21** (0.10)	−0.13 (0.09)	−0.16 (0.11)	−0.19 (0.12)	−0.09 (0.10)	−0.17* (0.09)	−0.20** (0.09)	−0.12 (0.09)
Veto players	−2.15** (1.13)	−2.[illegible]1** (1.[illegible]6)	−2.81** (1.16)	−2.31** ([illegible].12)	−2.91** (1.48)	−2.75** (1.46)	−2.03 (1.36)	−3.20** (1.26)	−3.11** (1.26)	−2.68 (1.25)
EU Defendant	−0.17 (0.40)	−0.[illegible]1 (0.[illegible]1)	0.03 (0.41)	−0.03 (0.41)	−0.15 (0.43)	−0.10 (0.44)	−0.54 (0.40)	−0.20 (0.40)	−0.14 (0.40)	−0.54 (0.39)
US Defendant	0.01 (0.36)	0.1[illegible] (0.[illegible]7)	0.13 (0.37)	0.21 (0.37)	−0.05 (0.38)	−0.02 (0.38)	−0.21 (0.37)	0.01 (0.36)	0.04 (0.36)	−0.09 (0.35)
Intermediate Import Dependence		0.6[illegible]** (0.[illegible]3)			0.63*** (0.24)			0.65** (0.22)		

(continued)

Table A.1 (continued)

	Baseline & time included	*Sector GVC included*	*Sector GVC included*	*Sector GVC included*	*Sector GVC included*	*Sector GVC included*	*Sector GVC included*	*Sector GVC included*	*Sector GVC included*	*Sector GVC included*
Import Dependence			0.45^{***} (0.14)			0.41^{**} (0.15)			0.43^{**} (0.13)	
Foreign inputs in exports				0.02^{*} (0.01)			0.02 (0.01)			0.02^{*} (0.01)
Num. obs.	138	138	138	138	132	132	132	137	137	137

$^{***}p < 0.01$, $^{**}p < 0.05$, $^{*}p < 0.1$
Standard errors in parentheses; all tests are two-tailed tests

Table A.2 Results from alternative specification of power asymmetry

	Baseline & time included	*Sector GVC included*	*Sector GVC included*	*Sector GVC included*	*Sector GVC included*	*Sector GVC included*	*Sector GVC included*	*Sector GVC included*	*Sector GVC included*	*Sector GVC included*
Power asymmetry	0.05	0.01	−0.02	−0.02						
	(0.10)	(0.10)	(0.10)	(0.11)						
FDI share					−0.01	−0.01	−0.01			
					(0.01)	(0.01)	(0.01)			
Export dependence								−0.01	−0.01	−0.01
								(0.01)	(0.01)	(0.01)
Def. democracy	0.07	0.09	0.08	0.05	0.10	0.09	0.09	0.11^{*}	0.10^{*}	0.12^{*}
	(0.05)	(0.05)	(0.05)	(0.07)	(0.07)	(0.07)	(0.07)	(0.06)	(0.06)	(0.06)
Issue complexity	0.83^{**}	0.95^{***}	0.91^{***}	1.09^{***}	0.86^{***}	0.82^{***}	0.72^{***}	0.89^{***}	0.85^{***}	0.75^{**}
	(0.24)	(0.24)	(0.24)	(0.24)	(0.25)	(0.25)	(0.25)	(0.25)	(0.24)	(0.24)
Sectoral value added	-0.18^{*}	-0.18^{*}	-0.21^{**}	−0.13	−0.16	−0.19	−0.09	-0.17^{*}	-0.20^{**}	−0.12
	(0.09)	(0.10)	(0.10)	(0.09)	(0.11)	(0.12)	(0.10)	(0.09)	(0.09)	(0.09)
Veto players	-2.15^{**}	-2.91^{**}	-2.81^{**}	-2.31^{**}	-2.91^{**}	-2.75^{**}	−2.03	-3.20^{**}	-3.11^{**}	−2.68
	(1.13)	(1.16)	(1.16)	(1.12)	(1.48)	(1.46)	(1.36)	(1.26)	(1.26)	(1.25)
EU defendant	−0.17	−0.01	0.03	−0.03	−0.15	−0.10	−0.54	−0.20	−0.14	−0.54
	(0.40)	(0.41)	(0.41)	(0.41)	(0.43)	(0.44)	(0.40)	(0.40)	(0.40)	(0.39)
US defendant	0.01	0.11	0.13	0.21	−0.05	−0.02	−0.21	0.01	0.04	−0.09
	(0.36)	(0.37)	(0.37)	(0.37)	(0.38)	(0.38)	(0.37)	(0.36)	(0.36)	(0.35)
Intermediate import dependence		0.67^{**}			0.63^{***}			0.65^{**}		
		(0.23)			(0.24)			(0.22)		

(continued)

Table A.2 (continued)

	Baseline & time included	*Sector GVC included*	*Sector GVC included*	*Sector GVC included*	*Sector GVC included*	*Sector GVC included*	*Sector GVC included*	*Sector GVC included*	*Sector GVC included*	*Sector GVC included*
Import dependence			0.45^{***} (0.14)			0.41^{**} (0.15)			0.43^{**} (0.13)	
Foreign inputs in exports				0.02^{*} (0.01)			0.02 (0.01)			0.02^{*} (0.01)
Num. obs.	138	138	138	138	132	132	132	137	137	137

$^{***}p < 0.01$, $^{**}p < 0.05$, $^{*}p < 0.1$
Standard errors in parentheses; all tests are two-tailed tests

Appendix B: The Details of the Disputes and the Corresponding Domestic Policy That Brought Compliance

A. B. Yildirim, *Value Chains and WTO Disputes*,
https://doi.org/10.1007/978-3-030-49094-2

DS number	*Description of the dispute*	*Defendant*	*Complainant*	*Domestic policy that brought compliance*
DS 7	Trade Description of Scallops	EU	Canada	Journal officiel de la République française "Avant-projet d'arrêté relatif aux dénominations de vente admises des Pectinidés"
DS 12	Trade Description of Scallops	EU	Peru	Journal officiel de la République française "Avant-projet d'arrêté relatif aux dénominations de vente admises des Pectinidés"
DS 14	Trade Description of Scallops	EU	Chile	Journal officiel de la République française "Avant-projet d'arrêté relatif aux dénominations de vente admises des Pectinidés"
DS 26	Measures Concerning Meat and Meat Products (Hormones)	EU	USA	European Parliament Directive 2003/74/EC
DS 27	Regime for the Importation, Sale and Distribution of Bananas	EU	Ecuador	Geneva Convention on Trade of Bananas
DS 27	Regime for the Importation, Sale and Distribution of Bananas	EU	Guatemala	Geneva Convention on Trade of Bananas
DS 27	Regime for the Importation, Sale and Distribution of Bananas	EU	Honduras	Geneva Convention on Trade of Bananas
DS 27	Regime for the Importation, Sale and Distribution of Bananas	EU	Mexico	Geneva Convention on Trade of Bananas
DS 27	Regime for the Importation, Sale and Distribution of Bananas	EU	USA	Geneva Convention on Trade of Bananas
DS 48	DS48—Measures Concerning Meat and Meat Products (Hormones)	EU	Canada	European Parliament Directive 2003/74/EC
DS 72	Measures Affecting Butter Products	EU	New Zealand	Council Regulation No. 2250/1999
DS 105	Regime for the Importation, Sale and Distribution of Bananas	EU	Panama	Geneva Convention on Trade of Bananas

(continued)

(continued)

DS number	*Description of the dispute*	*Defendant*	*Complainant*	*Domestic policy that brought compliance*
DS 141	Anti-Dumping Duties on Imports of Cotton-Type Bed Linen	EU	India	Council Regulation 1515/2001 and 1644/2001, which was successfully challenged, then Council Regulation (EC) No. 2239/2003
DS 174	Protection of Trademarks and Geographical Indications for Agricultural Products and Foodstuffs	EU	USA	Council Regulation (EC) No. 510/2006
DS 219	Anti-Dumping Duties on Malleable Cast Iron Tube or Pipe Fittings	EU	Brazil	Council Regulation (EC) No. 436/2004
DS 231	Trade Description of Sardines	EU	Peru	Commission Regulation EC 1181/2003, amending Regulation EEC 2136/89
DS 265	Export Subsidies on Sugar	EU	Australia	Several provisions: Regulation (EC) No. 1260/2001, No. 318/2006, Commission Regulation (EC) No. 769/2006, and amending Regulation (EC) No. 493/2006
DS 266	Export Subsidies on Sugar	EU	Brazil	Several provisions: Regulation (EC) No. 1260/2001, No. 318/2006, Commission Regulation (EC) No. 769/2006, and amending Regulation (EC) No. 493/2006
DS 269	Custom Classification of Frozen Boneless Chicken Cuts	EU	Brazil	Commission Regulation (EC) No. 949/2006
DS 283	Export Subsidies on Sugar	EU	Thailand, Australia	Several provisions: Regulation (EC) No. 1260/2001, No. 318/2006, Commission Regulation (EC) No. 769/2006, and amending Regulation (EC) No. 493/2006

(continued)

(continued)

DS number	*Description of the dispute*	*Defendant*	*Complainant*	*Domestic policy that brought compliance*
DS 286	Custom Classification of Frozen Boneless Chicken Cuts	EU	Thailand	Commission Regulation (EC) No. 949/2006
DS 290	Protection of Trademarks and Geographical Indications for Agricultural Products and Foodstuffs	EU	Australia	Council Regulation (EC) No. 510/2006
DS 291	Measures Affecting the Approval and Marketing of Biotech Products	EU	USA	N/A (bilateral dialogue established on 15 July 2009)
DS 292	Measures Affecting the Approval and Marketing of Biotech Products	EU	Canada	N/A (bilateral dialogue established on 15 July 2009)
DS 293	Measures Affecting the Approval and Marketing of Biotech Products	EU	Argentina	N/A (bilateral dialogue established on 15 July 2009)
DS 299	Countervailing Duties on Dynamic Random Access Memory Chips	EU	Korea, Republic of	Regulation (EC) No. 584/2006
DS 301	Measures Affecting Trade in Commercial Vessels	EU	Korea, Republic of	The challenged measure (TDM) expired in 2005 and was not renewed
DS 316	Measures Affecting Trade in Large Civil Aircraft	EU	USA	Non-compliance—proceedings ongoing
DS 337	Anti-Dumping Measures on Salmon	EU	Norway	Council Regulation (EC) No. 685/2008
DS 347	Measures Affecting Trade in Large Civil Aircraft	EU	USA	Non-compliance—proceedings ongoing
DS 375	Tariff Treatment of Certain Technological Products	EU	USA	Regulation (EU) No. 620/2011 amending Annex I to Council Regulation (EEC) No. 2658/78
DS 376	Tariff Treatment of Certain Technological Products	EU	Japan	Regulation (EU) No. 620/2011 amending Annex I to Council Regulation (EEC) No. 2658/78

(continued)

(continued)

DS number	*Description of the dispute*	*Defendant*	*Complainant*	*Domestic policy that brought compliance*
DS 377	Tariff Treatment of Certain Technological Products	EU	Taiwan	Regulation (EU) No. 620/2011 amending Annex I to Council Regulation (EEC) No. 2658/78
DS 397	Definitive Anti-Dumping Measures on Certain Iron or Steel Fasteners	EU	China	Regulation (EU) No. 620/2011 amending Annex I to Council Regulation (EEC) No. 2658/78
DS 405	Anti-Dumping Measures on Certain Footwear	EU	China	Regulation (EU) No. 765/2012 of the European Parliament and of the Council amending Council Regulation (EC) No. 1225/2009
DS 2	Standards for Reformulated and Conventional Gasoline	USA	Venezuela	Environmental Protection Agency (EPA) The Regulation of Fuels and Fuel Additives: Baseline Requirements for Gasoline Produced by Foreign Refiners on August 19, 1997, revising the requirements for imported conventional gasoline
DS 4	Standards for Reformulated and Conventional Gasoline	USA	Brazil	Environmental Protection Agency (EPA) The Regulation of Fuels and Fuel Additives: Baseline Requirements for Gasoline Produced by Foreign Refiners on August 19, 1997, revising the requirements for imported conventional gasoline
DS 24	Restrictions on Imports of Cotton and Man-Made Fiber Underwear	USA	Costa Rica	The challenged measure expired (and not renewed) by April 1997
DS 32	Measures Affecting Imports of Women's and Girls' Wool Coats	USA	India	61 Fed. Reg. (Federal Registry) Notification 64342

(continued)

(continued)

DS number	*Description of the dispute*	*Defendant*	*Complainant*	*Domestic policy that brought compliance*
DS 33	Measures Affecting Imports of Woven Wool Shirts and Blouses from India	USA	India	61 Fed. Reg. Notification 64342
DS 58	Import Prohibition of Certain Shrimp and Shrimp Products	USA	India	64 Fed. Reg. 36946 US Department of State revision of guidelines on the turtle/shrimp law
DS 58	Import Prohibition of Certain Shrimp and Shrimp Products	USA	Malaysia	64 Fed. Reg. 36946 US Department of State revision of guidelines on the turtle/shrimp law
DS 58	Import Prohibition of Certain Shrimp and Shrimp Products	USA	Pakistan	64 Fed. Reg. 36946 US Department of State revision of guidelines on the turtle/shrimp law
DS 58	Import Prohibition of Certain Shrimp and Shrimp Products	USA	Thailand	64 Fed. Reg. 36946 US Department of State revision of guidelines on the turtle/shrimp law
DS 99	Anti-Dumping Duty on Dynamic Random Access Memory Semiconductors (DRAMS) of One Megabit or Above from Korea	USA	Korea, Republic of	65 Fed. Reg. 59391
DS 138	Imposition of Countervailing Duties on Certain Hot-Rolled Lead and Bismuth Carbon Steel Products Originating in the United Kingdom	USA	EU	65 Fed. Reg. 13713

(continued)

(continued)

DS number	*Description of the dispute*	*Defendant*	*Complainant*	*Domestic policy that brought compliance*
DS 160	Section 110(5) of US Copyright Act	USA	EU	N/A (see: Congressional Research Service RL32014, stating that mutually agreed solution is ongoing without legislative changes)
DS 166	Definitive Safeguard Measures on Imports of Wheat Gluten from the European Communities	USA	EU	66 Fed. Reg. 18510 (The challenged measures were expired and not renewed. See: http://trade.ec.europa.eu/wtodispute/show.cfm?id=241&code=2)
DS 176	Section 211 Omnibus Appropriations Act of 1998	USA	EU	Non-compliance
DS 177	Safeguard Measure on Imports of Fresh, Chilled or Frozen Lamb from New Zealand	USA	New Zealand	Proclamation 7502 (revoking the safeguard measures)
DS 178	Safeguard Measure on Imports of Fresh, Chilled or Frozen Lamb from Australia	USA	Australia	Proclamation 7502 (revoking the safeguard measures)
DS 179	Anti-Dumping measures on Stainless Steel Plate in Coils and Stainless Steel Sheet and Strip from Korea	USA	Korea, Republic of	66 Fed. Reg. 45278
DS 184	Anti-Dumping Measures on Certain Hot-Rolled Steel Products from Japan	USA	Japan	67 Fed. Reg. 69186
DS 192	Transitional Safeguard Measure on Combed Cotton Yarn from Pakistan	USA	Pakistan	66 Fed. Reg. 56805 Committee for the Implementation of Textile Agreements (CITA) of Dept. of Commerce directive (to the Commissioner of Customs)

(continued)

(continued)

DS number	*Description of the dispute*	*Defendant*	*Complainant*	*Domestic policy that brought compliance*
DS 202	Definitive Safeguard Measures on Imports of Circular Welded Carbon Quality Line Pipe from Korea	USA	Korea, Republic of	68 Fed. Reg. 19578
DS 206	Anti-Dumping and Countervailing Measures on Steel Plate from India	USA	India	N/A
DS 212	Countervailing Measures Concerning Certain Products from the European Communities	USA	EU	Fed. Reg. 6519
DS 213	Countervailing Duties on Certain Corrosion-Resistant Carbon Steel Flat Products from Germany	USA	EU	69 Fed. Reg. 17131
DS 236	Preliminary Determinations with Respect to Certain Softwood Lumber from Canada	USA	Canada	Softwood Lumber Agreement of 2006
DS 248	Definitive Safeguard Measures on Imports of Certain Steel Products	USA	EU	Proclamation 7741
DS 249	Definitive Safeguard Measures on Imports of Certain Steel Products	USA	Japan	Proclamation 7741
DS 251	Definitive Safeguard Measures on Imports of Certain Steel Products	USA	Korea, Republic of	Proclamation 7741
DS 252	Definitive Safeguard Measures on Imports of Certain Steel Products	USA	China	Proclamation 7741
DS 253	Definitive Safeguard Measures on Imports of Certain Steel Products	USA	Switzerland	Proclamation 7741
DS 254	Definitive Safeguard Measures on Imports of Certain Steel Products	USA	Norway	Proclamation 7741

(continued)

(continued)

DS number	*Description of the dispute*	*Defendant*	*Complainant*	*Domestic policy that brought compliance*
DS 257	Final Countervailing Duty Determination with respect to certain Softwood Lumber from Canada	USA	Canada	Softwood Lumber Agreement of 2006
DS 258	Definitive Safeguard Measures on Imports of Certain Steel Products	USA	New Zealand	Proclamation 7741
DS 259	Definitive Safeguard Measures on Imports of Certain Steel Products	USA	Brazil	Proclamation 7741
DS 264	Final Dumping Determination on Softwood Lumber from Canada	USA	Canada	Softwood Lumber Agreement of 2006
DS 267	Subsidies on Upland Cotton	USA	Brazil	Public Law 112–155, see: USTR Press Release (April 6, 2010)
DS 268	Sunset Reviews of Anti-Dumping Measures on Oil Country Tubular Goods from Argentina	USA	Argentina	72 Fed. Reg. 34442
DS 277	Investigation of the International Trade Commission in Softwood Lumber from Canada	USA	Canada	Softwood Lumber Agreement of 2006
DS 282	Anti-Dumping Measures on Oil Country Tubular Goods (OCTG) from Mexico	USA	Mexico	N/A
DS 285	Measures Affecting the Cross-Border Supply of Gambling and Betting Services	USA	Antigua and Barbuda	Non-compliance
DS 296	Countervailing Duty Investigation on Dynamic Random Access Memory Semiconductors (DRAMS) from Korea	USA	Korea, Republic of	N/A

(continued)

(continued)

DS number	*Description of the dispute*	*Defendant*	*Complainant*	*Domestic policy that brought compliance*
DS 317	Measures Affecting Trade in Large Civil Aircraft	USA	EU	Non-compliance
DS 335	Anti-Dumping Measure on Shrimp from Ecuador	USA	Ecuador	72 Fed. Reg. 48257
DS 343	Measures Relating to Shrimp from Thailand	USA	Thailand	74 Fed. Reg. 14809
DS 344	Final Anti-Dumping Measures on Stainless Steel from Mexico	USA	Mexico	77 Fed. Reg. 29875, see: USTR Press Release (February 6, 2012)
DS 345	Customs Bond Directive for Merchandise Subject to Anti-Dumping/Countervailing Duties	USA	India	74 Fed. Reg. 14809
DS 353	Measures Affecting Trade in Large Civil Aircraft—Second Complaint	USA	EU	Non-compliance
DS 381	Measures Concerning the Importation, Marketing and Sale of Tuna and Tuna Products	USA	Mexico	N/A
DS 382	Anti-Dumping Administrative Reviews and Other Measures Related to Imports of Certain Orange Juice from Brazil	USA	Brazil	77 Fed. Reg. 23659; USITC 4311
DS 383	Anti-Dumping Measures on Polyethylene Retail Carrier Bags from Thailand	USA	Thailand	75 Fed. Reg. 48940
DS 384	Certain Country of Origin Labelling (Cool) Requirements	USA	Canada	Non-compliance
DS 386	Certain Country of Origin Labelling Requirements	USA	Mexico	Non-compliance

(continued)

(continued)

DS number	*Description of the dispute*	*Defendant*	*Complainant*	*Domestic policy that brought compliance*
DS 404	Anti-dumping Measures on Certain Shrimp from Viet Nam	USA	Viet Nam	77 Fed. Reg. 8101
DS 406	Measures Affecting the Production and Sale of Clove Cigarettes	USA	Indonesia	N/A (the complainant satisfied due to a deal that the US will not discriminate any other Indonesian tobacco products—e.g., cigars and cigarillos
DS18	Measures Affecting Importation of Salmon	Australia	Canada	Australia Quarantine and Inspection Service (Department of Agriculture) announcing Quarantine Policy Memorandum 1999/51, which is successfully challenged, and finally Ministerial Statement 17 May 2000
DS126	Subsidies provided to producers and exporters of automotive leather	Australia	USA	Government of Australia terminated the WTO-illegal grant contract to the Hower Leather Company on September 1999, which was successfully challenged by the USA and finally MAS on 31 July 2000 with temporary reduction of tariffs in various products, Howe's payments back to the Government of Australia—details available at Waarden, N. (2001) published in Australian International Law Journal
DS367	Measures Affecting the Importation of Apples from New Zealand	Australia	New Zealand	Australia Department of Agriculture, Fisheries and Forestry/Biosecurity Australia (report 2011/14)

(continued)

(continued)

DS number	*Description of the dispute*	*Defendant*	*Complainant*	*Domestic policy that brought compliance*
DS31	Certain Measures Concerning Periodicals	Canada	USA	BILL C-24: The Sales Tax and Excise Tax Amendments Act, 1999
DS70	Measures Affecting the Export of Civilian Aircraft	Canada	Brazil	N/A
DS103(113)	Measures Affecting the Importation of Milk and the Exportation of Dairy Products	Canada	USA	Canadian dairy commission the Comprehensive Agreement on Pooling of Milk Revenues
DS114	Patent Protection of Pharmaceuticals	Canada	EU	Repeal of SOR/93-134
DS139(142)	Certain Measures Affecting the Automotive Industry	Canada	Japan	Repeal of the Auto Pact (and the several provisions within)
DS170	Term of Patent Protection	Canada	USA	Bill S-17 with regard to Canada Patent Act
DS276	Measures Relating to Exports of Wheat and Treatment of Imported Grain	Canada	USA	Canada Transportation Act, Canada Grain Act
DS412(426)	Certain Measures Affecting the Renewable Energy Generation Sector	Canada	Japan	Ministry of Energy Directive MC 2013.1950
DS87(110)	Taxes on Alcoholic Beverages	Chile	EU	Ministerio de Haciendo (Ministry of Treasury and Commerce) Legislation Proposal on Beverage Tax adopted by the Congress January 2001)
DS207	Price Band System and Safeguard Measures Relating to Certain Agricultural Products	Chile	Argentina	N/A (see: USTR Foreign Trade Barrier Report 2008 that indicates the system was changed)
DS8 (10)	Taxes on Alcoholic Beverages	Japan	EU	Liquor Tax Law Amendment (October 1997) and a list of suspended tariffs

(continued)

(continued)

DS number	*Description of the dispute*	*Defendant*	*Complainant*	*Domestic policy that brought compliance*
DS76	Measures Affecting Agricultural Products	Japan	USA	Partial: Abolishment of testing requirements for entry (December 1999) and full revision by August 2001
DS245	Measures Affecting the Importation of Apples	Japan	USA	25 August 2005 amendments to Ministry of Agriculture, Forestry and Fisheries Notification No. 354 dated 10 March 1997 and Detailed Rules for Plant Quarantine Enforcement Regulation Concerning Fresh Fruit of Apple Produced in the United States of America dated 30 June 2004
DS336	Countervailing Duties on DRAM	Japan	Korea, Republic of	N/A (Bilateral dialogue established March 2009)
DS75	Taxes on Alcoholic Beverages	Korea, Republic of	EU	Liquor Tax Law (2000)
DS98	Definitive Safeguard Measure on Imports of Certain Dairy Products	Korea, Republic of	EU	N/A (Safeguard measures revoked through administrative procedures—see: notes on the DSB meeting 26 September 2000)
DS161	Measures Affecting Imports of Fresh, Chilled, and Frozen Beef	Korea, Republic of	USA	Ministry of Agriculture Notification 2000-82 and 2001-54
DS273	Measures Affecting Trade in Commercial Vessels	Korea, Republic of	EU	Measures expired and not renewed—see: notes on the DSB meeting 11 April 2005
DS312	AD Duties on Certain Imports of Paper from Indonesia	Korea, Republic of	Indonesia	N/A
DS391	Measures affecting the importation of bovine meat	Korea, Republic of	Canada	Notice 2012-3 of Korean Official Gazette

(continued)

(continued)

DS number	*Description of the dispute*	*Defendant*	*Complainant*	*Domestic policy that brought compliance*
DS132	AD Investigation of High Fructose Corn Syrup from the US	Mexico	USA	The challenged measures removed by Mexico in May 2002 (see: Kornis, M. (2006) United States Trade Commission)
DS204	Measures Affecting Telecommunications Services	Mexico	USA	Regulation on marketing of long distance and international long distance telecommunications services—Diario Oficial de la Federación—12 August 2005
DS295	Definitive Anti-Dumping Measures on Beef and Rice	Mexico	USA	Decree amending, supplementing and repealing various provisions of the Foreign Trade Act—Diario Oficial de la Federación 21 December 2006
DS308	Tax Measures on Soft Drinks and Other Beverages	Mexico	USA	Federal Revenue Law, published in December 2007 by Diario Oficial de la Federación
DS331	Anti-Dumping Duties on Steel Pipes and Tubes from Guatemala	Mexico	Guatemala	The challenged measures were removed in January 2008—Diario Oficial de la Federación—see: notes on the DSB meeting, 14 March 2008
DS341	Definitive Countervailing Duties on Olive Oil from the EU	Mexico	EU	The challenged measures were removed—domestic court ruling and the resolution published by the official gazette—see: notes on the DSB meeting, 11 December, 2008
DS34	Restrictions on Imports of Textile and Clothing Products	Turkey	India	Official Gazette 24626—Decision on the quantitative restrictions and tariff lines on items from India

(continued)

(continued)

DS number	*Description of the dispute*	*Defendant*	*Complainant*	*Domestic policy that brought compliance*
DS334	Measures Affecting the Importation of Rice	Turkey	USA	Several provisions: Official Gazette 26221, 26477, 26403
DS46	Export Financing Programme for Aircraft	Brazil	Canada	Banco Central Brasilia Resolution 2.799 (December 2000) Published in Relatorio 2000, also known as "Proex III"
DS332	Measures Affecting Imports of Retreaded Tyres	Brazil	EU	Portaria SECEX 24/2009 (See also: Brazil Supreme Court 24 June 2009
DS339	Measures Affecting Imports of Automobile Parts	China	EU	General Administration of Customs Order 58 and Order 185, repealing Decree 125: "Regarding the Announcement Abolishing the Rules for Determining Whether Imported Automotive Parts and Components Constitute Complete Vehicles" and "Decision to Abolish Administrative Rules on Importation of Automobile Parts Characterized as Complete Vehicles"

(continued)

(continued)

DS number	*Description of the dispute*	*Defendant*	*Complainant*	*Domestic policy that brought compliance*
DS339	Measures Affecting Imports of Automobile Parts	China	USA	General Administration of Customs Order 58 and Order 185, repealing Decree 125: "Regarding the Announcement Abolishing the Rules for Determining Whether Imported Automotive Parts and Components Constitute Complete Vehicles" and "Decision to Abolish Administrative Rules on Importation of Automobile Parts Characterized as Complete Vehicles"
DS339	Measures Affecting Imports of Automobile Parts	China	Canada	General Administration of Customs Order 58 and Order 185, repealing Decree 125: "Regarding the Announcement Abolishing the Rules for Determining Whether Imported Automotive Parts and Components Constitute Complete Vehicles" and "Decision to Abolish Administrative Rules on Importation of Automobile Parts Characterized as Complete Vehicles"
DS363	Measures Affecting Trading Rights and Distribution Services for Certain Publications and Audiovisual Entertainment Products	China	USA	Several provisions: See DSB meeting 22 February 2002
DS395	Measures Related to the Exportation of Various Raw Materials	China	Mexico	Zongshugonggao 2012 No. 63 and Gonggao 2012 No. 97

(continued)

(continued)

DS number	*Description of the dispute*	*Defendant*	*Complainant*	*Domestic policy that brought compliance*
DS395	Measures Related to the Exportation of Various Raw Materials	China	EU	Zongshugonggao 2012 No. 63 and Gonggao 2012 No. 97
DS395	Measures Related to the Exportation of Various Raw Materials	China	USA	Zongshugonggao 2012 No. 63 and Gonggao 2012 No. 97
DS413	Certain Measures Affecting Electronic Payment Services	China	USA	Non-compliance, see: DSB Meeting 16 March 2016. Attempt made by China via "People's Bank of China Announcement [2013] No. 7"
DS414	Countervailing and Anti-Dumping Duties on Grain Oriented Flat-rolled Electrical Steel from the United States	China	USA	(Contested measures expired by the circulation of panel reports)
DS50	Patent Protection for Pharmaceutical and Agricultural Chemical Products	India	USA	The Patents (Amendment) Act, 1999 (Gazette of India 26 March 1999)
DS146	Measures Affecting the Automotive Sector	India	USA	Dept. of Commerce Public Notice No. 31 (19 August 2002)
DS146	Measures Affecting the Automotive Sector	India	EU	Dept. of Commerce Public Notice No. 31 (19 August 2002)
DS54	Certain Measures Affecting the Automobile Industry	Indonesia	EU	Regulation No. 59/1999, Decrees of the Minister for Industry and Trade No. 275/1999 and No. 276/1999 and Decree of the Minister for Finance No. 344/1999
DS54	Certain Measures Affecting the Automobile Industry	Indonesia	Japan	Regulation No. 59/1999, Decrees of the Minister for Industry and Trade No. 275/1999 and No. 276/1999 and Decree of the Minister for Finance No. 344/1999

(continued)

(continued)

DS number	*Description of the dispute*	*Defendant*	*Complainant*	*Domestic policy that brought compliance*
DS54	Certain Measures Affecting the Automobile Industry	Indonesia	USA	Regulation No. 59/1999, Decrees of the Minister for Industry and Trade No. 275/1999 and No. 276/1999 and Decree of the Minister for Finance No. 344/1999
DS56	Measures Affecting Imports of Footwear, Textiles, Apparel and other Items	Argentina	USA	Decree 108/99
DS121	Safeguard Measures on Imports of Footwear	Argentina	EU	Contested measure expired by 25 February 2000
DS155	Measures Affecting the Export of Bovine Hides and the Import of Finished Leather	Argentina	EU	Several measures: Nota No. 52/01 SDGTLA, Nota No. 56/01 DI TECN, Nota No. 82/01 DI TECN, Dictamen No. 91/01 DV RTAG, Nota No. 88/01 DI TECN, Instrucción General No. 28/01 SDGLTA. Resolucion General AFIP 1048/2001 and 1100/2001
DS189	Definitive Anti-Dumping Measures on Imports of Ceramic Tiles	Argentina	EU	(Ministry of Production)Resolution 76/02
DS238	Definitive Safeguard Measure on Imports of Preserved Peaches	Argentina	Chile	(Ministry of the Economy) Resolution 91/2003
DS241	Definitive Anti-Dumping Duties on Poultry from Brazil	Argentina	Brazil	N/A
DS122	Anti-Dumping Duties on Angles, Shapes and Sections of Iron or Non-Alloy Steel and H Beams	Thailand	Poland	(Measures remained in place over 7 years, see, Davey, 2010, pp. 310)

(continued)

(continued)

DS number	*Description of the dispute*	*Defendant*	*Complainant*	*Domestic policy that brought compliance*
DS371	Customs and Fiscal Measures on Cigarettes from the Philippines	Thailand	Philippines	N/A
DS396	Taxes on Distilled Spirits	Philippines	EU	Republic Act No. 10351, "An Act Restructuring the Excise Tax on Alcohol and Tobacco Products" and Bureau of Internal Revenue (BIR) Revenue Regulation 17-2012
DS366	Indicative Prices and Restrictions on Ports of Entry	Colombia	Panama	Customs Authority Resolution No. 013518
DS464	Anti-Dumping and Countervailing Measures on Large Residential Washers	USA	Korea	Non-compliance
DS447	Meat and Animal Products	USA	Argentina	Federal Register Vol. 80 No. 127-37935
DS429	Shrimp	USA	Vietnam	United States Trade Representative (USTR), July 18, 2016 'Agreement between Vietnam and USA Frozen Warmwater Shrimp'
DS473	Biodiesel	EU	Argentina	Commission Implementing Regulation (EU) 2018/1570
DS480	Biodiesel	EU	Indonesia	Commission Implementing Regulation (EU) 2018/1570
DS482	Welded Pipe	Canada	Taiwan	Budget Implementation Act, 2017, No. 1 and Canada Border Services Agency (CBSA) and the Canadian International Trade Tribunal (CITT) Ruling of 29 September 2017

(continued)

(continued)

DS number	*Description of the dispute*	*Defendant*	*Complainant*	*Domestic policy that brought compliance*
DS431	Rare earths	China	USA	MOFCON Announcement on the Catalogue of Commodities Subject to Export License Administration in 2015—General Administration of Customs and Ministry of Commerce, Order No. (2014) 94, 31 December 2014. As well as Circular of Adjusting Export Duties on Some Products, by Customs Tariff Commission of the State Council, Order No. (2015) 3, 14 April 2015
DS432	Rare earths	China	EU	MOFCON Announcement on the Catalogue of Commodities Subject to Export License Administration in 2015—General Administration of Customs and Ministry of Commerce, Order No. (2014) 94, 31 December 2014. As well as Circular of Adjusting Export Duties on Some Products, by Customs Tariff Commission of the State Council, Order No (2015) 3, 14 April 2015

(continued)

(continued)

DS number	Description of the dispute	Defendant	Complainant	Domestic policy that brought compliance
DS433	Rare earths	China	Japan	MOFCON Announcement on the Catalogue of Commodities Subject to Export License Administration in 2015—General Administration of Customs and Ministry of Commerce, Order No. (2014) 94, 31 December 2014. As well as Circular of Adjusting Export Duties on Some Products, by Customs Tariff Commission of the State Council, Order No. (2015) 3, 14 April 2015
DS427	Broiler products	China	USA	Non-compliance
DS425	X-ray products	China	EU	MOFCOM Announcement No. 9 of 2014 on Ceasing Anti-dumping Taxes Against Imports of X-ray Security Inspection Equipment Originated in the EU
DS479	Commercial Light Vehicles	Russia	EU	AD duties expired and not renewed on 15 June 2018
DS468	Passenger vehicles	Ukraine	Japan	Interdepartmental Commission on International Trade decision of 10 September 2015 No. SP-335/2015/4442-06

Cases that were taken out of the sample:

Disputes in which the defendants were exonerated

- (EU) DS135: Asbestos dispute with Canada
- (EU) DS62: Computer Equipment dispute
- (EU) DS69: Tariff rate quota on poultry products from Brazil
- (EU) DS369/400/401: The seal dispute: EU was exonerated on most accounts, and the final implementing measures are being examined as to their WTO-compatibility
- (EU) DS442 AD Measures on Imports of Certain Fatty Alcohols from Indonesia
- (EU) DS486 Countervailing Measures on Certain Polyethylene Terephthalate from Pakistan
- (USA) DS152: Sections 301-310 of the Trade Act of 1974
- (USA) DS165: Import measures for certain products from the EU
- (USA) DS194: Measures treating export restraints as subsidies
- (USA) DS221: Section 129 (c)(1) of Uruguay trade agreements act
- (USA) DS243: Rules of origin for Textiles and Apparel products
- (USA) DS244: Sunset reviews of AD duties on steel from Japan
- (USA) DS320: Continued suspension of obligations in the EU-Hormones dispute
- (USA) DS392: Certain measures affecting imports of poultry from China
- (USA) DS399: Measures affecting imports of tire from China
- (USA) DS491: Anti-Dumping and Countervailing Measures on Certain Coated Paper from Indonesia
- (Japan) DS44: Measures Affecting Consumer Photographic Film and Paper
- (Korea) DS163: Measures Affecting Government Procurement
- (Canada) DS321: Continued Suspension of Obligations in the EU—Hormones Dispute
- (Brazil) DS22: Measures Affecting Desiccated Coconut
- (India) DS360: Additional and Extra-Additional Duties on Imports from the United States
- (China) DS440: Anti-Dumping and Countervailing Duties on Certain Automobiles from the United States
- (India) DS360: Additional and Extra-Additional Duties on Imports from the United States.

Horizontal disputes that are not included in the dataset

EU

- DS246: Conditions for the Granting of Tariff Preferences to Developing Countries
- DS315: Selected Customs Matters.

USA

- DS38: The Cuban Liberty and Democratic Solidarity Act
- DS39: Tariff Increases on Products from the European Communities
- DS88/95: Measure Affecting Government Procurement
- DS108: Tax Treatment for "Foreign Sales Corporations"
- DS118: Harbour Maintenance Tax
- DS136/162: Anti-Dumping Act of 1916
- DS186: Section 337 of the Tariff Act of 1930 and Amendments thereto
- DS200: Section 306 of the Trade Act 1974 and Amendments thereto
- DS217: Continued Dumping and Subsidy Offset Act of 2000 (Byrd Amendment)
- DS224: US Patents Code
- DS 294: Laws, Regulations and Methodology for Calculating Dumping Margins (Zeroing)
- DS319: Section 776 of the Tariff Act of 1930
- DS379: Definitive Anti-Dumping and Countervailing Duties on Certain Products from China
- DS437: Countervailing Duty Measures on Certain Products from China
- DS449: Countervailing and Anti-Dumping Measures on Certain Products from China
- DS471: Certain Methodologies and their Application to Anti-Dumping Proceedings Involving China.

Others

- DS90: India—Quantitative Restrictions on Imports of Agricultural, Textile and Industrial Products
- DS362: China—Measures Affecting the Protection and Enforcement of Intellectual Property Rights
- DS472: Brazil—Certain Measures Concerning Taxation and Charges
- DS485: Russia—Tariff Treatment of Certain Agricultural and Manufacturing Products
- DS477/478: Indonesia—Importation of Horticultural Products, Animals and Animal Products.

Calculation of Compliance from Different Perspectives

Example (1) The defendant complies after a panel ruling.

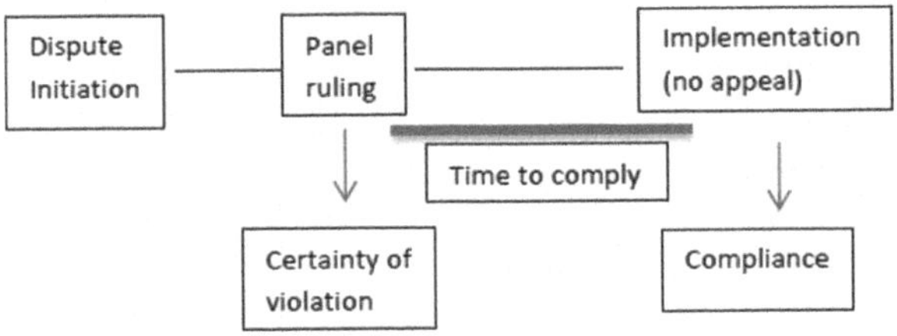

Example (2) The defendant complies after an appellate body ruling.

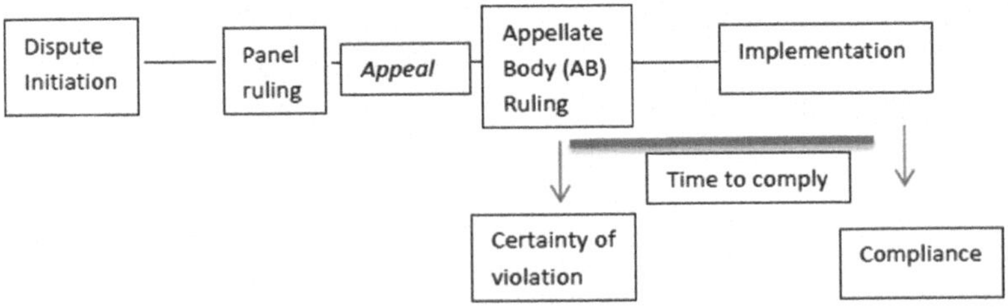

Example (3) The defendant complies after an appellate body ruling, which is contested and overruled.

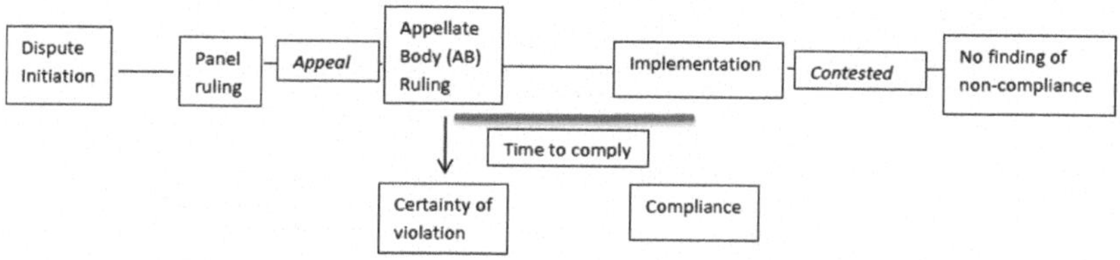

Example (4) The defendant allegedly complies after an appellate body ruling but found to be non-compliant, and introduces a new measure.

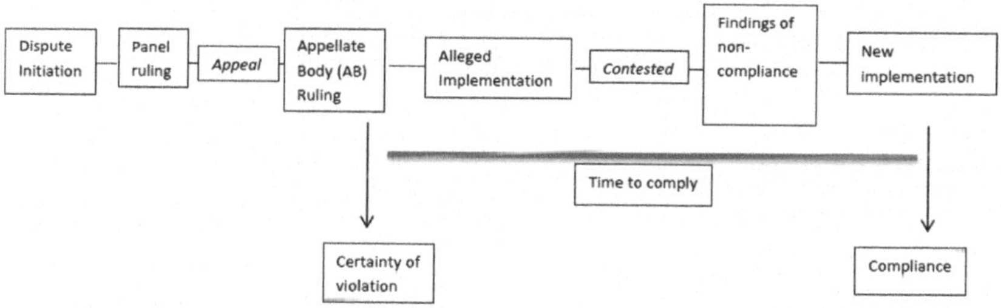

WTO Panel Stage and Possible Compliance Options Employed in the Study (Different Visualization)

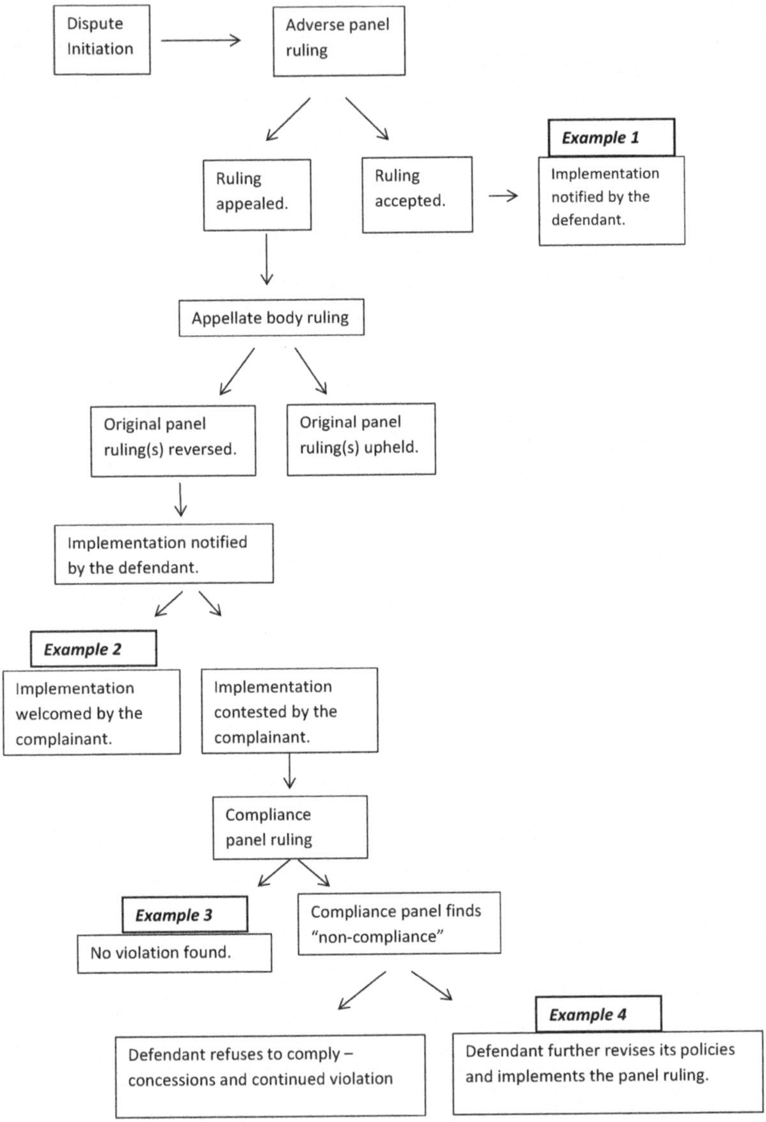

Coding of Henisz' Political Constraints dataset for the EU

Indicators' presence and the corresponding coding:

	L1 (Lower house of the legislature)	*L2 (Upper house of the legislature)*	*E (Executive)*	*F (Federal entitites)*	*J (Judiciary)*
Presence	Yes	Yes	Yes	Yes	Yes
Corresponding entity	European Parliament	Council of the European Union	European Union Commission	Member States	European Court of Justice

Alignment of the Executive and the Parliament (Aligne_L1)

This indicator is measured by looking at the corresponding European Commissions' approval rate by the parliament and secondly the composition of the Commission from the ruling parties.

1994–1999 (5th European Parliament):
Santer Commission: 417 votes for, 104 against
Majority coalition: PES–EPP
Commission composition: 9 (PES) 7 (EPP-AD) 2 (ELDR) 2 (Independent).

1999–2004 (6th European Parliament):
Prodi Commission: (Increase in the power of the Commission/executive with the Amsterdam Treaty and Nice Treaty, as well as the increase in the number of portfolios)
Prodi Commission: 510 votes for, 51 against
Majority coalition: PES–EPP/ED
Commission composition: 1999–2003: 10 (PES) 5 (EPP-ED) 2 (ELDR) 1 (Greens) 1 (Independent)
2004: 8 (PES) 9 (EPP-ED) 6 (ELDR) 1 (Greens) 6 (Independent).

2004–2009 (7th European Parliament):
Barosso Commission: 478 votes for, 84 votes against
Majority coalition: PES–EPP
Commission composition: 8 (EPP) 8 (ELDR) 6 (PES) 4 (Independents) 1 (Alliance).

2009–2014 (8th European Parliament):
2nd Barosso Commission: 488 vote for, 137 against
Majority coalition: EPP and S&D
Commission composition: 13 (EPP) 7 (ALDE/ELDR) 7(PES).

Alignment of the Executive and the Council (Aligne_l2)

This measure considers the executive and the council to be aligned if the ruling coalition in the legislative is also of the same party of the executive. In the Council of the European Union, there is no ruling coalition in the traditional sense, and the Council in essence furthers the interests of the EU member states, therefore an alignment between the Commission and the Council is considered nonexistent.

Alignment of the Parliament and the Council (Alignli_l2)

Similar to the executive EU Commission alignment with the Council, the EU Parliament and the council represent different constituencies. Therefore, their "alignment" in the traditional sense of policymaking is not expected.

Legislative Fractionalization

For the Council, this indicator is measured by looking at the number of member states present for the Council and the weighed voting rules. Thus, fractionalization increases with the number of member states whose consent is necessary and the increase in the qualified majority voting.

For the parliament, fractionalization increases with the number of parties in the parliament and the number of parties in a coalition.

Council:
1995–2004: 15 member states, 64 votes out of 87 are required
2004: 25 member states, 88 votes out of 124 is required
2004–2006: New, much more complex weighed criteria. 232 votes out of 321, and/or 62%
2009 Onwards: 27 member states, continuing with the 62% rule.

1994–1999 (5th European Parliament)
Total of 9 parties (+ the independents). PES (Social Democrats) and EPP (Conservatives and Christian Democrats) could pass legislation with a coalition, with a total of 355 seats out of 567 (62%)
1999–2004 (6th European Parliament)
Total of 8 parties (+ the independents). PES (Social Democrats) and EPP–ED (Conservatives and Christian Democrats) could pass legislation with a coalition, with a total of 413 seats out of 626 (66%).
2004–2009 (7th European Parliament)
Total of 8 parties (+ the independents). PES and EPP could pass legislation with a coalition, with a total of 485 seats out of 732 (66%)
10 New member states
2009–2014 (8th European Parliament)
Total of 7 parties (+ the independents). S&D and EPP could pass legislation with a coalition, with a total of 449 seats out of 736 (61%)
2 New member states.

Law and Order

This measure assumes a high number of 5.5 for the EU across the board.

References

Alter, K. 2003. Resolving or Exacerbating Disputes? The WTO's New Dispute Resolution System. *International Affairs* 79 (4): 783–800.

Amador, João, and S. Cabral. 2014. Global Value Chains Surveying Drivers and Measures. Working Paper 1739 (2014). European Central Bank (ECB), Frankfurt. Available at https://www.ecb.europa.eu/pub/pdf/scpwps/ecbwp1739.en.pdf?13f6d86f40a3c60325f27cbc08a18742. Accessed on March 22, 2016.

American Consumers for Affordable Homes. 2003. Treatment of Sector 201 Duties and Countervailing Duties, statement released on October 9, 2003. Available at http://enforcement.trade.gov/download/canada-softwood-lumber/acah-softwood-lumber-cmts.pdf. Accessed on March 21.

Antràs, Pol, and Elhanan Helpman. 2004. Global Sourcing. *Journal of Political Economy* 112 (3): 552–580.

Antràs, Pol, and Robert W. Staiger. 2012. Offshoring and the Role of Trade Agreements. *American Economic Review* 102 (7): 3140–3183.

Axelrod, Robert. 1984. *The Evolution of Cooperation*. New York: Basic.

Axelrod, R., and R. Keohane. 1985. Achieving Cooperation Under Anarchy: Strategies and Institutions. *World Politics* 38 (1): 226–254.

Baccini, L., and S.Y. Kim. 2012. Preventing Protectionism: International Institutions and Trade Policy. *The Review of International Organizations* 7 (4): 369–398.

Baccini, L., A. Dür, and M. Elsig. 2018. Intra-Industry Trade, Global Value Chains, and the Political Economy of Preferential Trade Liberalization. *International Studies Quarterly* 62 (2): 329–340.

A. B. Yildirim, *Value Chains and WTO Disputes*,
https://doi.org/10.1007/978-3-030-49094-2

Baccini, Leonardo, Pablo M. Pinto, and Stephen Weymouth. 2017. The Distributional Consequences of Preferential Trade Liberalization: Firm-Level Evidence. *International Organization* 71 (2): 373–95.

Baccini, Leonardo, Pablo M. Pinto, and Stephen Weymouth. 2018. The Distributional Consequences of Preferential Trade Liberalization: Firm-Level Evidence. *International Organization* 71 (2): 373–395.

Bagwell, K., P. Mavroidis, and R. Staiger. 2004. The Case for Tradable Remedies in WTO Dispute Settlement. Discussion Paper No. 0405-05. New York, NY: Department of Economics, Columbia University.

Baldwin, R. 2012. Global Supply Chains: Why They Emerged, Why They Matter, and Where They Are Going. Working Paper 2012-01. Fung Global Institute, Hong Kong.

Baldwin, R. 2014. WTO 2.0: Governance of 21st Century Trade. *The Review of International Organizations* 9 (2): 261–283.

Barrett, S. 2007. *Why Cooperate? The Incentive to Supply Global Public Goods*. Oxford: Oxford University Press (Oxford Scholarship Online).

Baumgartner, Aldo. 2001. Statement on the Amendment of the Patent Act. Speech, Ottawa. *Proceedings of the Standing Senate Committee on Banking, Trade and Commerce*, Canadian Senate, March 21.

Bechtel, M., and T. Sattler. 2015. What Is Litigation in the World Trade Organization Worth? *International Organization* 69 (2): 375–403.

Belzile, A. 2003. *Statement on the World Trade Organization's Decision on the Canadian Dairy Export Policy*. Speech, Proceedings of the Standing Committee on Agriculture and AgriFood, 18 March, Ottowa.

Bentham, J. 1800. The Manual of Political Economy. In *The Collected Works of Jeremy Bentham*, ed. Michael Quinn. Oxford: Oxford University Press.

Berkhout, J., B. Carroll, C. Braun, A.W. Chalmers, T. Destrooper, D. Lowery, S. Otjes, and A. Rasmussen. 2015. Interest Organizations Across Economic Sectors: Explaining Interest Group Density in the European Union. *Journal of European Public Policy* 22 (4): 462–480.

Bernard, A., and B. Jensen. 1995. Exporters, Jobs, and Wages in U.S. Manufacturing: 1976–1987. Brookings Papers on Economic Activity, Microeconomics, 67–119.

Bernard, A., B. Jensen, and P.K. Schott. 2006. Survival of the Best Fit: Exposure to Low-Wage Countries and the (Uneven) Growth of U.S. Manufacturing Plants. *Journal of International Economics* 68 (1): 219–237.

Bernard, A., B. Jensen, and P.K. Schott. 2009. Importers, Exporters, and Multinationals: A Portrait of Firms in the U.S. That Trade Goods. In *Producer Dynamics*, ed. Timothy Dunne, J. Bradford Jensen and Mark J. Roberts. Chicago: University of Chicago Press.

Bernhagen, P. 2008. Business and International Environmental Agreements: Domestic Sources of Participation and Compliance by Advanced Industrialized Democracies. *Global Environmental Politics* 8 (1): 78–110.

Blanchard, E., C. Bown, and R. Johnson. 2016. Global Supply Chains and Trade Policy. Policy Research Working Paper 7536. World Bank, Washington, DC. https://openknowledge.worldbank.org/handle/10986/23702.

Bonomo, D. 2014. Hitting Where It Hurts: Retaliation Requests in the WTO. VoxEU, Centre for Economic and Policy Research. Available at http://voxeu.org/article/retaliation-wto. Accessed on June 22, 2017.

Bown, C. 2004. On the Economic Success of GATT/WTO Dispute Settlement. *The Review of Economics and Statistics* 86 (3): 811–823.

Bown, C. 2009. *Self-Enforcing Trade: Developing Countries and WTO Dispute Settlement*. Washington: Brookings Institution Press.

Bown, C. 2017. Will the Proposed U.S. Border Tax Provoke WTO Retaliation From Trading Partners? Peterson Institute for International Economics Policy Paper. Available at https://piie.com/publications/policy-briefs/will-proposed-us-border-tax-provoke-wto-retaliation-trading-partners. Accessed on June 21, 2017.

Bown, C., and K. Reynolds. 2014. Trade Flows and Trade Disputes. Policy Research Working Paper 6979. Development Research Team, World Bank, Washington.

Box-Steffensmeier, J., D. Reiter, and C. Zorn. 2003. Nonproportional Hazards and Event History Analysis in International Relations. *Journal of Conflict Resolution* 47 (1): 33–53.

Brewster, R. 2012. Reputation in International Relations and International Law Theory. In *Interdisciplinary Perspectives on International Law and International Relations –The State of the Art*, ed. Jeffrey Dunoff and Mark Pollack. Cambridge: Cambridge University Press.

Brewster, R., and A. Chilton. 2014. Supplying Compliance: Why and When the United States Complies with WTO Rulings. *Yale Journal of International Law* 39 (2): 201–247.

Briggs, J., S. Laaksonen-Craig, K. Niquidet, and C. van Kooten. 2005. Resolving Canada-U.S. Trade Disputes in Agriculture and Forestry: Lessons from Lumber. Working Paper 2005-03. Resource Economics and Policy Analysis Research Group. University of Victoria.

Bronckers, M., and F. Baetens. 2013. Reconsidering Financial Remedies in WTO Dispute Settlement. *Journal of International Economic Law* 16 (2): 281–311.

Burney, I. 2003. *Statement on the World Trade Organization's Decision on the Canadian Dairy Export Policy*. Speech, Proceedings of the Standing Committee on Agriculture and AgriFood, 18 March, Ottowa.

Busch, M. 2000. Bargaining in the Shadow of the Law: Early Settlement in GATT/WTO Disputes. *Fordham International Law Journal* 24: 158–172.

Busch, M., and K. Pelc. 2010. The Politics of Judicial Economy at the World Trade Organization. *International Organization* 64 (2): 257–259.

Busch, M., and E. Reinhardt. 2000. Bargaining in the Shadow of the Law: Early Settlement in GATT/WTO Disputes. *Fordham International Law Journal* 24: 158–172.

Busch, M., and E. Reinhardt. 2003. Transatlantic Trade Conflicts and GATT/WTO Dispute Settlement. In *Transatlantic Economic Disputes: The EU, The US, and the WTO*, ed. E. Petersmann and M. Pollack. Oxford: Oxford University Press.

Busch, M., and E. Reinhardt. 2006. Three's a Crowd: Third Parties and WTO Dispute Settlement. *World Politics* 58 (3): 446–477.

Busch, M., E. Reinhardt, and G. Shaffer. 2009. Does Legal Capacity Matter? A Survey of WTO Members. *World Trade Review* 8 (4): 559–577.

Bush, G. 2002. Announcement on the Temporary Safeguards for the Steel Industry. United States White House Office of the Press Secretary. Available at https://georgewbush-whitehouse.archives.gov/infocus/steel/.

Cattaneo, O., G. Gereffi, and C. Staritz. 2010. *Global Value Chains in a Postcrisis World: A Development Perspective*. Washington, DC: The World Bank. Available at http://issuu.com/world.bank.publications/docs/9780821384992. Accessed on May 22, 2017.

Charron, M. 2005. Lumber I to IV. History of the Canada—U.S. Softwood Lumber Dispute. Canadian Parliamentary Research Service report TIPS-134E published on December 19.

Chase, K. 2003. Economic Interests and Regional Trading Arrangements: The Case of NAFTA. *International Organization* 57 (1): 137–174.

Chaudoin, S., J. Kucik, and K. Pelc. 2016. Do WTO Disputes Actually Increase Trade? *International Studies Quarterly* 0: 1–13. Advanced online publication. Available at http://isq.oxfordjournals.org/content/early/2016/04/15/isq.sqw009.

Chayes, A., and A.H. Chayes. 1993. On Compliance. *International Organization* 47 (2): 175–205.

Chen, Yu. 2015. EU-China Solar Panels Trade Dispute: Settlement and challenges to the EU. European Institute for Asian Studies. Available at http://www.eias.org/eu-asia-at-a-glance/eu-china-solar-panels-trade-dispute-settlement-and-challenges-for-the-eu-june-2015/. Accessed on February 10, 2017.

Commission of the European Communities (CEC). 2002. The European Commission's Strategy to Respond to the US Decision to Impose Protectionist duties on steel imports. MEMO/02/59, March 18.

Commission of the European Communities (CEC). 2004. US Byrd Amendment—WTO Says Eight WTO Members May Retaliate Against the US—Joint

Press statement by Brazil, Canada, Chile, the EU, India, Japan, Korea, and Mexico. MEMO IP/04/1055, August 31.

Consuming Industries Trade Action Coalition. 2002. Statement 'Tariff Exclusion Process Will Not Solve Steel Consumers' Struggles, December 4.

Conti, J. 2010. *Between Law and Diplomacy: The Social Contexts of Disputing at the World Trade Organization*. Oxford: Oxford University Press.

Cox, T., D. Le Roy, and E. Goddard. 2001. Dairy Disputes in North America: A Case Study. In *Trade Liberalization under NAFTA: Report Card on Agriculture, Proceedings of the Sixth Agricultural and Food Policy Systems Information Workshop*, ed. R.M.A. Loyns, K. Meilke, R.D. Knutson, and A. Yunez-Naude, 253–282. San Diego. March 2000.

Dai, X. 2005. Why Comply? The Domestic Constituency Mechanism. *International Organization* 59 (2): 363–398.

Dai, X. 2008. Effectiveness of International Environmental Institutions. *Global Environmental Politics* 8 (3): 154–158.

Davey, A. 2005. Evaluating WTO Dispute Settlement: What Results Have Been Achieved Through Consultations and Implementation of Panel Reports? Research Paper 05-19. Chicago, IL: College of Law, University of Illinois.

Davey, W.J. 2010. The WTO Dispute Settlement System: How Have Developing Countries Fared?. In *Is the World Trade Organization Attractive Enough for Emerging Economies?* ed. Z. Drabek. London: Palgrave Macmillan.

Davis, C. 2012. *Why Adjudicate: Enforcing Trade Rules in the WTO*. Princeton, NJ: Princeton University Press.

Davis, C., and K. Pelc. 2015. Cooperation in Hard Times: Self-Restraint of Trade Protection. *Journal of Conflict Resolution*. https://doi.org/10.1177/0022002715595699.

Davis, C., and Y. Shirato. 2007. Firms, Governments, and WTO Adjudication: Japan's Selection of WTO Disputes. *World Politics* 59 (2): 274–313.

Dean, J.M., K.C. Fung, and Z. Wang. 2007. Measuring the Vertical Specialization in Chinese Trade. Working Paper, No. 2007-01-A. U.S. International Trade Commission, Office of Economics.

De Bièvre, D., and A. Dür. 2005. Constituency Interests and Delegation in European and American Trade Policy. *Comparative Political Studies* 38 (10): 1271–1296.

Dispute Settlement Understanding (DSU), Dispute Settlement Rules: Understanding on Rules and Procedures Governing the Settlement of Disputes, Marrakesh Agreement Establishing the World Trade Organization, Annex 2.

Dixon, W.J. 1993. Democracy and the Management of International Conflict. *Journal of Conflict Resolution* 37 (1): 42–68.

Dossani, R., and M. Kenney. 2003. Lift and Shift; Moving the Back Office to India. *Information Technologies and International Development* 1 (2): 21–37.

Dunoff, J., and M. Pollack. 2012. International Law and International Relations: Introducing an Interdisciplinary Dialogue. In *Interdisciplinary Perspectives on International Law and International Relations: The State of the Art*, ed. Jeffrey Dunoff and Mark Pollack. Cambridge: Cambridge University Press.

Eckhardt, J. 2011. Firm Lobbying and EU Trade Policy Making: Reflections on the Anti-Dumping Case Against Chinese and Vietnamese Shoes (2005–2011). *Journal of World Trade* 45 (5): 965–991.

Eckhardt, J. 2015. *Business Lobbying and Trade Governance: The Case of EU-China Relations*. New York and Basingstoke: Palgrave Macmillan.

Eckhardt, J., and A. Poletti. 2016. The Politics of Global Value Chains: Import Dependent Firms and EU-Asia Trade Agreements. *Journal of European Public Policy*. https://doi.org/10.1080/13501763.2015.1085073.

Eckhardt, J., and M. Elsig. 2015. Support for International Trade Law: The US and the EU Compared. *International Journal of Constitutional Law* 13 (4): 966–986.

Efron, B. 1977. The Efficiency of Cox's Likelihood Function for Censored Data. *Journal of the American Statistical Association* 72 (359): 557–565.

Elms, D., and P. Low. 2013. Global Value Chains in a Changing World, Introduction, Switzerland: World Trade Organization. Available at https://www.wto.org/english/res_e/booksp_e/aid4tradeglobalvalue13_e.pdf. Accessed on June 20, 2020.

Escaith, H., L. Nannette, and S. Miroudot. 2010. International Supply Chains and Trade Elasticity in Times of Global Crisis. Economic Research and Statistics, World Trade Organization, January 30.

Fearon, J. 1994. Domestic Political Audiences and the Escalation of International Disputes. *The American Political Science Review* 88 (3): 577–592.

Fergusson, I. 2011. United States-Canada Trade and Economic Relationship: Prospects and Challenges. U.S. Congressional Research Service report RL33087. Available at https://fas.org/sgp/crs/row/RL33087.pdf. Accessed on March 2 2016.

Fox, J. and S. Weisberg. 2011. *An R Companion to Applied Regression*, 2nd ed. Thousand Oaks, CA: Sage.

Francois, J., and L. Baughman. 2001. Estimated Economic Effects of Proposed Import Relief Remedies for Steel. Report Prepared by Trade Partnership Worldwide LLC. Available at http://tradepartnership.com/reports/estimated-economic-effects-of-proposed-import-relief-remedies-for-steel-2001/.

Gereffi, G. 1994. The Organization of Buyer-Driven Global Commodity Chains: How U.S. Retailers Shape Overseas Production Networks. In *Commodity Chains and Global Capitalism*, ed. G. Gereffi and M. Korzeniewicz, 95–122. Westport, CT: Praeger.

Gereffi, G. 1999. International Trade and Industrial Upgrading in the Apparel Commodity Chain. *Journal of International Economics* 48 (1): 37–70.

Gereffi, G., J. Humphrey, and T. Sturgeon. 2005. The Governance of Global Value Chains. *Review of International Political Economy* 12 (1): 78–104.

Gifford, D. 2004. *Government Policy Towards Innovation in the United States, Canada, and the European Union as Manifested in Patent, Copyright, and Competition Laws*. University of Minnesota Law School SMU Law Review paper 1339 (2004). Available at http://scholarship.law.umn.edu/faculty_articles/333. Accessed on June 20, 2020.

Gilligan, M. 1997. Lobbying as a Private Good with Intra-Industry Trade. *International Studies Quarterly* 41: 455–474.

Goldberg P., A. Khandelwal, N. Pavcnik, and P. Topalova. 2010. Imported Intermediate Inputs and Domestic Product Growth: Evidence from India. *The Quarterly Journal of Economics* 125 (4): 1727–1767.

Goldstein, J. 1996. International Law and Domestic Institutions: Reconciling North American "Unfair" Trade Laws. *International Organization* 50 (4): 541–564.

Goldstein, Judith, and Lisa L. Martin. 2000. Legalization, Trade Liberalization, and Domestic Politics: A Cautionary Note. *International Organization* 54 (3): 603–632.

Goldstein, J., and R. Steinberg. 2008. Negotiate or Litigate? Effects of WTO Judicial Delegation on US Trade Politics. *Law and Contemporary Problems* 71 (1): 257–282.

Greenspan, Alan. 2003. Speech Given at the "Economic Outlook" Hearing Before the Joint Economic Committee of the United States Congress, May 21.

Grossman, G., and E. Helpman. 1994. Protection for Sale. *The American Economic Review* 84 (4): 833–850.

Grossman, G., and E. Helpman. 2001. *Special Interest Politics*. Cambridge: MIT Press.

Guzman, A. 2008. *How International Law Works: A Rational Choice Theory*. Oxford: Oxford University Press.

Guzman, A., and B. Simmons. 2002. To Settle or Empanel? An Empirical Analysis of Litigation and Settlement at the WTO. *Journal of Legal Studies* 31 (1): 205 235.

Guzman, A., and B. Simmons. 2005. Power Plays and Capacity Constraints: The Selection of Defendants in World Trade Organization Disputes. *Journal of Legal Studies* 34 (2): 557–598.

Hafner-Burton, E. 2005. Trading Human Rights: How Preferential Trade Agreements Influence Government Repression. *International Organization* 59 (593): 629.

Hathaway O.A. 2002. Do Human Treaties Make a Difference? *The Yale Law Journal* 111 (8): 1935–2034.

Hellenier, G.K. 1977. Transnational Enterprises and the New Political Economy of U.S. Trade Policy. *Oxford Economic Papers* 29 (1): 102–116. Available at http://econpapers.repec.org/article/oupoxecpp/v_3a29_3ay_3a1977_3ai_3a1_3ap_3a102-16.htm. Accessed on March 3, 2017.

Helpman, E., M. Marc, and S. Yeaple. 2004. Export Versus FDI with Heterogeneous Firms. *The American Economic Review* 94 (1): 300–316.

Henisz, W.J. 2011. Political Constraints Database, data and code accessed via http://www-management.wharton.upenn.edu/henisz/.

Henkin, Louis. 1979. *How Nations Behave*. Washington: Council on Foreign Relations Publications.

Hiscox, M.J. 2001. Class Versus Industry Cleavages: Inter-Industry Factor Mobility and the Politics of Trade. *International Organization* 55: 1–46.

Hoekman, B., and P. Mavroidis. 2000. WTO Dispute Settlement, Transparency and Surveillance. *World Economy* 23 (4): 527–542.

Hoffman, T., and S.Y. Kim. 2009. The Political Economy of Compliance in WTO Disputes. Paper Presented at Political Economy of International Organizations Conference, Geneva, Switzerland.

Horn, H., H. Nordström, and P. Mavroidis. 1999. Is the Use of the WTO Dispute Settlement System Biased? Discussion Paper 2340. London: Centre for Economic Policy Research.

Horn, H., L. Johannesson, and P. Mavroidis. 2011. The WTO Dispute Settlement System 1995–2010: Some Descriptive Statistics. *Journal of World Trade* 45 (6): 1107–1138.

Hudec, R. 1993. *Enforcing International Trade Law: The Evolution of the Modern GATT Legal System*. Salem: Butterworth Legal.

Humphrey, J., and H. Schmitz. 2002. How Does Insertion in Global Value Chains Affect Upgrading in Industrial Clusters? *Regional Studies* 36 (9): 1017–1027.

Jacobs, M. 2016. Smart Threats and Success in WTO Dispute Settlement: The Bush Steel Tariffs. E-International Relations, March 24, 2016. Available at http://www.e-ir.info/2016/03/24/smart-threats-and-success-in-wto-dispute-settlement-the-bush-steel-tariffs/. Accessed on June 20, 2020.

Jensen, B., D. Quinn, and S. Weymouth. 2013. Global Supply Chains, Currency Undervaluation, and Firm Protectionist Demands. Working Paper 19239. National Bureau of Economic Research, Cambridge, MA. Available at http://www.nber.org/papers/w19239. Accessed on September 17, 2015.

Jensen, B., D. Quinn, and S. Weymouth. 2015. The Influence of Firm Global Supply Chains and Foreign Currency Undervaluations on US Trade Disputes. *International Organization* 69: 913–947.

Johnson, R.C., and G. Noguera. 2012. Accounting for Intermediates: Production Sharing and Trade in Value Added. *Journal of International Economics* 86 (2): 224–236.

Jordan, M. 2005. *The Politics of Drug Patenting in Canada*. Masters dissertation, University of Saskatchewan.

Katzenstein, P.J. 1985. *Small States in World Markets: Industrial Policy in Europe*. Cornell Studies in Political Economy. Ithaca, NY: Cornell University Press.

Keohane, R. 1984. *After Hegemony: Cooperation and Discord in the World Political Economy*. Princeton, NJ: Princeton University Press.

Keohane, R., and J. Nye. 1977. *Power and Interdependence: World Politics in Transition*. New York: Brown University Press.

Keon, J. 2001. *Statement on the amendment of the Patent Act*. Speech, House of Commons Standing Committee on Industry, Science, and Technology, 17 May, Ottowa.

Kim, In Song. 2017. Political Cleavages within Industry: Firm-level Lobbying for Trade Liberalization. *American Political Science Review* 111.1: 1–20.

Kim, In Song, Helen Milner, Thomas Bernauer, Iain Osgood, Gabrielle Spilker, and Dustin Tingley. 2016. Firms' Preferences over Multidimensional Trade Policies: Global Production Chains, Investment Protection and Dispute Settlement Mechanisms. Working Paper.

Kim, S.Y. 2012. Protectionism During Recession: Is This Time Different? *The Political Economist* 9 (2): 6–8.

Kim, S.Y. 2015. Regionalization in Search of Regionalism: Production Networks and Deep Integration Commitments in Asia's PTAs. In *The Purpose, Design, and Effects of Preferential Trade Agreements*, ed. Andreas Dür and Manfred Elsig. Cambridge: Cambridge University Press.

Kim, In Song, Helen V. Milner, Thomas Bernauer, Iain Osgood, Gabriele Spilker, and Dustin Tingley. 2019. Firms and Global Value Chains: Identifying Firms' Multidimensional Trade Preferences. *International Studies Quarterly* 63 (1): 153–167.

Krikorian, J. 2005. Planes, Trains and Automobiles: The Impact of the WTO "Court" on Canada in Its First Ten Years. *Journal of International Economic Law* 8 (4): 921–975.

Koremenos, B. 2012. Institutionalism and International Law. In *Interdisciplinary Perspectives on International Law and International Relations—The State of the Art*, ed. Jeffrey Dunoff and Mark Pollack. Cambridge: Cambridge University Press.

Krasner, S.D. 1983. *International Regimes*. Ithaca, NY: Cornell University Press.

Krugman, P. 1981. Intraindustry Specialization and the Gains from Trade. *Journal of Political Economy* 89 (5): 959–973.

Lanz, Rainer, and Sebastien Miroudot. 2011. Intra-Firm Trade: Patterns, Determinants and Policy Implications. Working Paper 114. Trade Policy Papers. Organization for Economic Cooperation and Development (OECD) Publishing, Paris. Available at http://www.oecd-ilibrary.org/trade/intra-firm-trade_5kg9p39lrwnn-en. Accessed on April 12, 2016.

Lapid, Y. 1989. The Third Debate: On the Prospects of International Theory in a Postpositivist Era. *International Studies Quarterly* 33: 235–254.

Lawrence, R. 2007. The United States and the WTO Dispute Settlement System. Council on Foreign Relations, Greenberg Center for Geoeconomic Studies Special Report. Available at https://www.cfr.org/report/united-states-and-wto-dispute-settlement-system. Accessed on June 19, 2017.

Leuiliette, Timothy. 2003. Impact of the Section 201 Safeguard Action on Certain Steel Products. Speech given before the U.S. House of Representatives Committee on Ways and Means Subcommittee on Trade, March 26.

Levy, D.L. 2008. Political Contestation in Global Production Networks. *Academy of Management Review* 33 (4): 943–963.

Lexchin, J. 2001. Globalization, Trade Deals, and Drugs: Heads the Industry Wins Tails Canada Loses. *Canada Centre for Policy Alternatives Briefing Paper* 2 (8). November 2001.

Lexchin, J. 2005. Intellectual Property Rights and the Canadian Pharmaceutical Marketplace: Where Do We Go From Here? *International Journal of Health Service* 35 (2): 237–256.

Lobby Canada. 2001. *Registration and Organization Information: Rx&D*. Office of the Commissioner of Lobbying of Canada. Available at https://lobbycanada.gc.ca/app/secure/ocl/lrs/do/vwRg?cno=12328®Id=491884#regStart. Accessed on June 20, 2020.

Los, Bart, Marcel P. Timmer, and Gaaitzen de Vries. 2014. How Global Are Global Value Chains? A New Approach to Measure International Fragmentation. *Journal of Regional Science* 55: 66–92.

Manger, Mark. 2009. *Investing in Protection: The Politics of Preferential Trade Agreements Between North and South*. Cambridge: Cambridge University Press.

Manger, Mark. 2012. Vertical Trade Specialization and the Formation of North-South PTAs. *World Politics* 64 (4): 622–658.

Mansfield, E., and H. Milner. 2017. The Domestic Politics of Preferential Trade Agreements in Hard Times. *World Trade Review*. https://doi.org/10.1017/S1474745617000428.

Mansfield, E., H. Milner, and Jon Pevehouse. 2007. Vetoing Co-operation: The Impact of Veto Players on Preferential Trading Agreements. *British Journal of Political Science* 37 (3): 403–432.

Mansfield, E., H. Milner, and Peter Rosendorff. 2002. Why Democracies Cooperate More: Electoral Control and International Trade Agreements. *International Organization* 56 (3): 477–513.

Marshall, M., and K. Jaggers. 2002. Polity IV Project: Regime Characteristics and Transitions, 1800–2007. Available at http://www.systemicpeace.org/polity/polity4.htm. Accessed on April 12, 2016.

Martin, L. 1992. Interests, Power, and Multilateralism. *International Organization* 46 (4): 765–792.

Martin, L. 2000. *Democratic Commitments: Legislatures and International Cooperation*. Princeton: Princeton University Press.

Mavroidis, Petros. 2000. Remedies in the WTO Legal System: Between a Rock and a Hard Place. *European Journal of International Law* 11 (4): 763–813.

Mavroidis, Petros. 2012. On Compliance in the WTO: Enforcement Among Unequal Disputants. Briefing Paper No. 4. Geneva: CUTS International.

Melitz, Marc. 2003. The Impact of Trade on Intra-Industry Reallocations and Aggregate Industry Productivity. *Econometrica* 71 (6): 1695–1725.

Messer, A., J. Berkhout, and D. Lowery. 2011. The Density of the EU Interest System: A Test of the ESA Model. *British Journal of Political Science* 41 (01): 161–190.

Milner, H. 1987. Resisting the Protectionist Temptation: Industry and the Making of Trade Policy in France and the United States During the 1970s. *International Organization* 41 (4): 639–665.

Milner, H. 1997. *Interests, Institutions, and Information: Domestic Politics and International Relations*. Princeton: Princeton University Press.

Miroudot, S., R. Lanz, and A. Ragoussis. 2009. Trade in Intermediate Goods and Services. OECD Trade Policy Working Paper No. 93, November 3. Available at https://www.oecd.org/trade/its/44056524.pdf. Accessed on May 22 2017.

Moravcsik, A. 1997. Taking Preferences Seriously: A Liberal Theory of International Politics. *International Organization* 51 (4): 513–553.

Moravcsik, A. 2012. Liberal Theories of International Law, In. *Interdisciplinary Perspectives on International Law and International Relations—The State of the Art*, ed. Jeffrey L. Dunoff and Mark A. Pollack. Cambridge: Cambridge University Press.

Morrow, J. 2007. When Do States Follow the Laws of War? *American Political Science Review* 101 (3): 559–572.

Olson, M. 1965. *The Logic of Collective Action: Public Goods and the Theory of Groups*. Cambridge, MA: Harvard University Press.

Orefice, G., and N. Rocha. 2014. Deep Integration and Production Networks: An Empirical Analysis. *The World Economy* 37 (1): 106–136.

Organization for Economic Cooperation and Development (OECD). 1993. Glossary for Industrial Organisation Economics and Competition Law. Available at https://www.oecd.org/regreform/sectors/2376087.pdf. Accessed on February 15, 2016.

Organization for Economic Cooperation and Development (OECD). 2013. Interconnected Economies: Benefiting from Global Value Chains. Policy Synthesis Report. https://www.oecd.org/sti/ind/interconnected-economies-GVCs-synthesis.pdf. Accessed on February 11, 2017.

Organization for Economic Cooperation and Development (OECD). 2014. Global Value Chains, Challenges, Opportunities, and Implications for Policy, Report prepared and submitted for the G-20 Trade Minister's Meeting, Sydney, Australia, July 2014. Available at https://www.oecd.org/tad/gvc_report_g20_july_2014.pdf. Accessed on April 12, 2016.

Osgood, I. 2016. The Breakdown of Industrial Opposition to Trade: Firms, Product Variety and Reciprocal Liberalization. *World Politics*. https://doi.org/10.1017/S0043887116000174.

Park, A. 1999. *Examination of Canada's Trade Objectives and the Forthcoming Agenda of the World Trade Organization (WTO)*. Speech, Proceedings of the Standing Committee on Foreign Affairs and International Trade, 25 March, New Brunswick.

Patterson, E. 2001. The US-EU Banana Dispute. *American Society of International Law (ASIL) Insight Paper* 6: 4. Available at https://www.asil.org/insights/volume/6/issue/4/us-eu-banana-dispute. Accessed on January 2, 2017.

Pauwelyn, Joost. 2000. Enforcement and Countermeasures in the WTO: Rules are Rules-Toward a More Collective Approach. *American Journal of International Law* 94 (2): 335–347.

Pauwelyn, Joost. 2019. WTO Dispute Settlement System Post-2019: What to Expect? *Journal of International Economic Law* 22 (3): 297–321. Available at https://doi.org/10.1093/jiel/jgz024.

Peritz, L. 2016. When are International Institutions Effective? The Impact of Domestic Veto Players on Compliance with WTO Rulings. Paper Presented at the 9th Annual Meeting of the Political Economy of International Organizations. Salt Lake City, Utah.

Poletti, A. 2017. Robert Keohane: The Promises of Cooperation. In *Classics in International Relations*, ed. Filippo Andreatta. Bologna: Il Mulino publishing.

Poletti, A., and D. De Bièvre. 2014. Political Mobilization, Veto Players, and WTO Litigation: Explaining European Union Responses in Trade Disputes. *Journal of European Public Policy* 21 (8): 1181–1198.

Poletti, A., and D. De Bièvre. 2016. *Judicial Politics and International Cooperation: From Disputes to Deal-Making at the World Trade Organization*. Colchester: ECPR Press.

Poletti, A., D. De Bièvre, and T. Chatagnier. 2015. Cooperation in the Shadow of WTO Law: Why Litigate When You Can Negotiate? *World Trade Review* 14 (S1): S33–S58.

Popper, K. 1934. *The Logic of Scientific Inquiry*. London: Routledge.

Producteurs de lait du Québec (PLQ). 2000. *Annual Report: Training and Information*, On file with author.

Producteurs de lait du Québec (PLQ). 2013. *2013 Annual Report: 30 Years, Proud of Our Collective Achievements*, On file with author.

Przeworski, A., and H. Teune. 1970. *The Logic of Comparative Social Inquiry*. New York: Wiley.

Putnam, R. 1988. Diplomacy and Domestic Politics: The Logic of Two-Level Games. *International Organization* 42 (3): 427–460.

Ramondo, N., V. Rappoport, and K. Ruhl. 2011. Horizontal vs Vertical FDI: Revisiting Evidence from U.S. Multinationals, Working Paper. Available at https://ideas.repec.org/p/ste/nystbu/11-12.html. Accessed on May 22, 2017.

Read, R. 2005. The EU-US WTO Steel Dispute: Political Economy of Protection and the Efficacy of the WTO Dispute Settlement Understanding. In *The WTO and the Regulation of International Trade: Recent Trade Disputes Between the European Union and the United States*, ed. Nicholas Perdikis and Robert Read, 135–175. Cheltenham : Edward Elgar.

Reif, L. 2007. Desperate Softwood Lumber Companies? The Canada-US Softwood Lumber Dispute and NAFTA Chapter 11. *Alberta Law Review* 45 (2): 357–380.

Rodrik, D. 1998. Why Do More Open Economies Have Bigger Governments? *Journal of Political Economy* 106 (5): 997–1032.

Ruggie, John Gerard. 1982. International Regimes, Transactions, and Change: Embedded Liberalism in Postwar Economic Order. *International Organization* 36 (2): 379–415.

Rus, T. 2007. The Short, Unhappy life of the Byrd Amendment, N.Y.U. *Journal of Legislation and Public Policy* 10 (2): 427–443.

Saint-Jacques, J. 2000. *Information Session on the Canadian Dairy Exports under the World Trade Organization (WTO)*. Speech, Proceedings of the Standing Committee on Agriculture and AgriFood, 24 February, Ottowa.

Sattler, T., and T. Bernauer. 2011. Gravitation or Discrimination? Determinants of litigation at the World Trade Organization. *European Journal of Political Research* 50 (2): 143–167.

Sattler, Thomas, Gabriele Spilker, and Thomas Bernauer. 2014. Does WTO Dispute Settlement Enforce or Inform? *British Journal of Political Science* 44 (4): 877–902 (Published online in 2013).

Schmidt, B. 2002. On the History and Historiography of International Relations. In *Hand of International Relations*, ed. Walter Carlsnaes, Thomas Eisse, and Beth Simmons, 3–22. London: Sage.

Shaffer, G. 2003. *Defending Interests: Public-Private Partnerships in WTO Litigation*. Washington: Brookings Institution Press.

Shaffer, G., M. Elsig, and S. Puig. 2016. The Law and Politics of WTO Dispute Settlement. In *The Politics of International Law*, ed. Wayne Sandholtz and Christopher Whytock. Oxford: Oxford University Press.

Shoyer, A., E. Solovy, and A. Koff. 2005. Implementation and Enforcement of Dispute Settlement Decisions. In *The World Trade Organization: Legal,*

Economic and Political Analysis, ed. M. Plummer and A. Appleton. New York, NY: Springer.

Simmons, B.A. 2000. International Law and State Behavior: Commitment and Compliance in International Monetary Affairs. *American Political Science Review* 94 (4): 819–835.

Simmons, B.A. 2009. *Mobilizing Human Rights: International Law in Domestic Politics*. Cambridge: Cambridge University Press.

Slaughter, A. 1995. International Law in a World of Liberal States. *European Journal of International Law* 6 (1): 503–538.

Smith, A. 1776. *An Inquiry into the Nature and Causes of the Wealth of Nations*. Edinburgh: William Strahan.

Snidal, D. 1985. Coordination Versus Prisoners' Dilemma: Implications for International Cooperation and Regimes. *American Political Science Review* 79 (4): 923–942.

Spilker, Gabriele. 2012. Compliance with WTO Dispute Rulings. Working Paper 2011-25. National Centre of Competence in Research Trade Regulation, Zurich, Switzerland.

Sturgeon, T., and G. Gereffi. 2010. Measuring Success in the Global Economy: Technological Learning, Industrial Upgrading, and Business Function Outsourcing in Global Value Chains. Transnational Corporations, 17: 4. Available at https://unctad.org/en/docs/diaeiia200910a1_en.pdf. Accessed on June 20, 2020.

Sturgeon, T., and Olga Memedovic. 2010. Mapping Global Value Chains: Intermediate Goods Trade and Structural Change in the World Economy. United Nations Industrial Development Organization Working Paper 05/2010. Available at http://www.unido.org/fileadmin/media/documents/pdf/Publications/110905/WP052010_E.pdf. Accessed on April 29, 2017.

Tomz, M. 2007. Domestic Audience Costs in International Relations: An Experimental Approach. *International Organization* 61 (4): 821–840.

Trachtman, J. 2012. Open Economy Law. In *Interdisciplinary Perspectives on International Law and International Relations—The State of the Art*, ed. Jeffrey L. Dunoff and Mark A. Pollack. Cambridge: Cambridge University Press.

Tsebelis, G. 2002. *Veto Players: How Political Institutions Work*. Princeton: Princeton University Press.

United States Department of Agriculture (USDA). 2000. *Canadian Dairy Industry Spokesman Speculates New Dairy Regime Won't Be WTO Compliant*. Global Agricultural Information Network Report CA0124, August 2000, On file with author.

United States Department of Agriculture (USDA). 2001. *Canada's Subsidized Dairy Exports: The Issue of WTO Compliance*. Special article prepared by Economic Research Service, August 2001, On file with author.

United States Coalition for Fair Lumber Imports (USLC). 2002a. WTO: Canadian Subsidies Exist, Subsidy to be Recalculated. Statement released on September 27.

United States Coalition for Fair Lumber Imports (USLC). 2002b. U.S. Lumber Industry Seeks Negotiated Offset to Unfair Trade. Statement released on December 17.

United States Coalition for Fair Lumber Imports (USLC). 2003. Canadian Lumber Proposal Warrants Further Discussion. Statement released on July 31.

United Nations Conference on Trade and Development (UNCTAD). 2013. World Investment Report, Global Value Chains: Investment and Trade for Development. United Nations Publication: Switzerland. Available at https://unctad.org/en/PublicationsLibrary/wir2013_en.pdf. Accessed on June 20, 2020.

United States International Trade Administration (USITA). 2016. U.S. Export Fact Sheet—Export Statistics. Available at http://trade.gov/press/press-releases/2016/export-factsheet-040516.pdf. Accessed on February 2, 2017.

United States International Trade Commission (USITC). 2001. Determinations Concerning Impact of Imports of Steel on U.S. Industry, October 23. https://www.usitc.gov/press_room/news_release/2001/er1023y1.pdf.

United States International Trade Commission (USITC). 2003. Steel-Consuming Industries: Competitive Conditions With Respect to Steel Safeguard Measures (Investigation No. 332-452).

Verheul, S. 2003. *Statement on the World Trade Organization's Decision on the Canadian Dairy Export Policy*. Speech, Proceedings of the Standing Committee on Agriculture and AgriFood, 18 March, Ottawa.

Veeman, M. 2000. Preparing for the Challenges and Opportunities Beyond 2000 Through Future Dairy Policy in Canada: Implications for Production and Trade. *Advances in Dairy Technology* 12: 331–341.

Vinet, S. 2000. *Information Session on the Canadian Dairy Exports under the World Trade Organization (WTO)*. Speech, Proceedings of the Standing Committee on Agriculture and AgriFood, 24 February, Ottawa.

Von Stein, J. 2012. The Engines of Compliance. In *Synthesizing Insights from International Law and International Relations*, ed. Jeffrey Dunoff and Mark Pollack. Cambridge: Cambridge University Press.

Wilson, B. 2007. Compliance by WTO Members with Adverse WTO Dispute Settlement Rulings: The Record to Date. *Journal of International Economic Law* 10 (2): 397–403.

World Trade Organization. 2004. *Handbook on the WTO Dispute Settlement System*. Cambridge: Cambridge University Press.

World Trade Organization. 2016. *Resolving Trade Disputes Between WTO Members*. Geneva: Switzerland. https://www.wto.org/english/thewto_e/20y_e/dispute_brochure20y_e.pdf. Accessed on June 20, 2020.

Yildirim, Aydin. 2017. Domestic Political Implications of Global Value Chains: Explaining EU Responses to Litigation at the World Trade Organization. *Comparative European Politics*.

Yildirim, Aydin. 2018. Firms' Integration into Value Chains and Compliance with Adverse WTO Panel Rulings. *World Trade Review* 17 (1): 1–31.

Yildirim, Aydin, Arlo Poletti, Tyson Chatagnier, and Dirk De Bievre. 2018. Internationalization of Production and Compliance in WTO Disputes. *Review of International Organizations* 13: 49–75.

Young, A.R. 2010. Effective Multilateralism on Trial: EU Compliance with WTO Law. In *The EU's Presence in International Organisations*, ed. S. Blavoukos and D. Bourantonis, vol. 67, 114–131. European Union Series: Routledge advances in European politics. Abingdon, UK: Routledge.

Zangl, Bernhard. 2008. Judicialization Matters! A Comparison of Dispute Settlement Under GATT and the WTO. *International Studies Quarterly* 52 (4): 825–854.

Zhang, D. 2007. *The Softwood Lumber War. Politics, Economics, and the Long U.S.-Canadian Trade. Dispute*. New York: Routledge.

Zhang, Daowei, and David Laband. 2003. From Senators to the President: Solve the Lumber Problem or Else. *Public Choice* 123 (3): 393–410.

Zimmermann, T. 2006. Negotiating the Review of the World Trade Organization Dispute Settlement Understanding. Cameron May.

Zoellick, R. 2003. Press Briefing by US Trade Representative Zoellick on Ending the Temporary Steel Safeguards. Washington: The White House Office of the Press Secretary. Available at http://iipdigital.usembassy.gov/st/english/texttrans/2003/12/20031204164450yessedo0.718197.html#ixzz45cv7YfiB. Accessed on April 12, 2016.

Index

A. B. Yildirim, *Value Chains and WTO Disputes*,
https://doi.org/10.1007/978-3-030-49094-2

U

V

W

The manufacturer's authorised representative in the EU is Springer Nature Customer Service Centre GmbH, Europaplatz 3, 69115 Heidelberg, Germany. If you have any concerns regarding our products, please contact ProductSafety@springernature.com

Printed and bound by CPI Group (UK) Ltd, Croydon, CR0 4YY
05/10/2026
02227715-0002